FARMING
IN A FLOWERPOT

FARMING IN A FLOWERPOT

by Alice Skelsey

New and Revised Edition
formerly
Cucumbers in a Flowerpot

WP

Workman Publishing Company
New York

Workman Publishing Company, Inc.
231 East 51 Street
New York, New York 10022

First printing April 1975

Illustrations by Ed Rahn Studio
Cover design by Paul Hanson
Cover photograph by Jerry Darvin
Cover illustration by Isadore Seltzer

Typeset by Trade Composition
Printed and bound by the George Banta Company
Manufactured in the United States of America

To Gloria and Fred Huckaby—
Master Gardeners in and around the house . . .
as generous with help in learning and
writing about container farming as with the
harvests from their gardens.
Beautiful people.

CONTENTS

WHAT'S IN STORE FOR THE CITY FARMER

A packet of seeds, a pot of soil, a spot of sunshine—that's all you need to become a city farmer. Why be content with philodendron and ivy just because you live in an apartment? You should be growing fruit and vegetables instead!

Yes, you *can* farm in flowerpots. You can have your "houseplants" and eat them, too. Horticulturists have developed fruits and vegetables specially suited to growing in containers—midget, miniature, dwarf and doubledwarf varieties that take only a minimal amount of space and attention.

A tender young spring carrot tastes little like its store-bought cousin. Strawberries eaten minutes after leaving your high-rise "patch" are definitely sweeter, both in flavor and in the satisfaction of knowing you grew them yourself. Potted tomatoes, peppers and lettuce are beautiful to behold and offer a ready supply of salads right from your own balcony. All are possible for apartment dwellers or anyone with limited garden space.

While the economics of farming in flowerpots may be a toss-up for most crops (tomatoes, green peppers and cucumbers often more than pay their way, though), who could set a monetary value on the pleasure to be derived from growing your own. Nothing short of moving to the country could do more to freshen the spirits and surroundings of the cramped city-dweller. Whether you're an inveterate "green-thumber" or entirely inexperienced, you'll find growing your own fruits and vegetables at home a rewarding and delicious experience.

All sorts of convenience products new on the market make gardening anything but a chore. You will find pre-packaged soil mixes that are far more reliable than ordinary garden soil; plants that can be moved from one environment to another (pot and all) without ever disturbing a root; and carefully formulated fertilizers for "instant" feedings. With all kinds and varieties of plants for the city farmer to try, excitement and suspense are built into each new season. Could you recognize the beautiful gray-green leaves and lavender flowers of the eggplant? Do you really recall the flavor of a fresh-picked tomato? Equipped with a patio, balcony, doorstep or even a windowsill, plus sunlight for a good part of the day, your "farm" will know no limits. So tell your African violets, geraniums and philodendrons to move over and make room, and try a few new crops each spring.

SEVEN STEPS TO FARMING IN A FLOWERPOT

1. Choosing Containers for Your Crops

To get the most out of your "land," it's important to match the container to the crop. Obviously, a container should be large enough to hold the plant and its fruit when it reaches maturity. But sometimes it is difficult to judge just how big a plant will grow, seed packet information notwithstanding, Just one leaf-lettuce plant, for example, while starting out as the tiniest of seeds and emerging as the most fragile of seedlings, can, nonetheless, grow to overflow a gallon container. An eggplant will need a container as large as a half-bushel basket (four gallons), not so much for the bushlike plant but to accommodate its fruit, which is large and heavy.

On the other hand, some plants do not do well in large containers. They actually seem to prefer a pot that is small in relation to their size at maturity. A large tomato plant can thrive in a two-gallon container provided it is well-balanced and won't topple when the plant grows top-heavy. A miniature tomato plant can be grown in an eight- or 10-inch flowerpot.

Since decisions on container size cannot always be based on advance knowledge of the mature plant and its fruit, you must learn from your own observations of the plant's growth habits. The encouraging aspect of such "by-guess-and-by-golly" gardening is that it takes little additional effort or expense to adjust crops and containers from year to year as you gain experience. The novice with no idea of where to start should first consult the recommendations for each fruit and vegetable in the individual sections devoted to them. The following table will also be of help in visualizing the approximate capacity of different type containers, most of which are on hand in every household.

	quart	half-gallon	gallon	10-gallon	20-gallon	30-gallon
Milk carton	✓	✓	✓			
One-pound coffee can	✓					
Two-pound coffee can		✓				
Plastic ice cream carton	✓	✓				
Plastic bleach container	✓	✓	✓			
Garbage can				✓	✓	✓

Ordinary red clay pots are the preference of many gardeners. These range in size from two to 14 inches (diameter measured across the inside top) and have corresponding saucers for catching drainage water. They are widely available, decorative, relatively inexpensive, and ideal for most plants.

Here's a table of sizes and approximate prices. The latter will vary somewhat in different localities; garden centers in discount stores often offer the lowest prices but not always the widest selection of sizes.

SIZE, CAPACITY, AND PRICE OF CLAY POTS			
Diameter Inside Top	*Approximate Soil Content*	*Pot*	*Price Saucer*
2 inches	1/3 cup	$ .15	$ .15
2½ inches	2/3 cup	.23	.23
3 inches	1 cup	.23	.23
4 inches	2½ cups	.29	.24
5 inches	4½ cups	.47	.39
6 inches	2½ quarts	.67	.57
7 inches	3 quarts	.76	.68
8 inches	1 gallon	1.49	.93
9 inches	1½ gallons	2.07	1.36
10 inches	2¼ gallons	2.65	1.75
12 inches	3½ gallons	4.75	3.25
14 inches	6 gallons	8.65	3.64

Styrofoam pots which look almost like their clay counterparts are also available and are comparable in size and price. These are fairly new on the market, and while some advantages are claimed for them (lightweight, good insulation against heat), city farmers may find they tip over easily and cannot be used for taller, heavy-fruited plants such as tomatoes. They would probably be most satisfactory as a liner or container within a container. Tin cans will also work if holes are punched in the sides of the can, near the bottom, to allow for drainage.

For trees, select a container large enough to last for a number of years, so you won't have to go looking for a new one every season. Some trees, such as orange, lemon and lime, do well in small containers. A gallon-size pot will last for at least three or four years. Other fruit trees, such as dwarf peaches, have a large root system—as large or larger than the above-ground part of the tree when it's first purchased. Such a tree must obviously start out in a tub roomy enough to accommodate its roots. Large wooden tubs are beautiful but somewhat expensive. For redwood, figure about $1 per inch of the tub's diameter. Ten dollars for a 10-inch diameter tub, $25 for a 24-inch. Teakwood or cypress are other possibilities. All of these woods are rot-resistant; soil can be placed into them directly. If a wooden crate or a barrel or box made of pine or oak is selected, the inside should be coated with creosote, an asphalt paint or a commercial preparation called Cuprinol to prevent rot. Because wooden containers over 12 inches in diameter can become quite heavy (an 18-inch diameter tub filled with soil could weigh more than 200 pounds), a roller platform should be placed beneath them.

These platforms—simply an inch-thick board with ball-bearing casters attached—are available for $5 to $10.

Barrels can be used for berries. Reproductions of old packing barrels are now widely available. A barrel is a bit of a project to prepare (see Strawberries, page 96) and is heavy when filled but makes a wonderful "patch" that will last for years.

Growers with some yard space or convenient access to a roof might consider building a raised bed for a vegetable garden that can really be cultivated and coddled. Caution: Check first with the building owner or superintendent before rushing out for supplies; the weight of wet soil and containers can be substantial. One three-foot-wide, six-foot-long

bed filled with soil 10 inches deep could weigh
more than 1,000 pounds. Raised beds can be con-
structed from 2 × 12-inch redwood boards rein-
forced at the corners, as illustrated. Although the
length of the bed will, of course, depend on the
available space, its width should be at least three
feet, sufficient to accommodate two or three rows of
radishes, lettuce, beets, carrots or onions—a sort
of mini-truck farm.

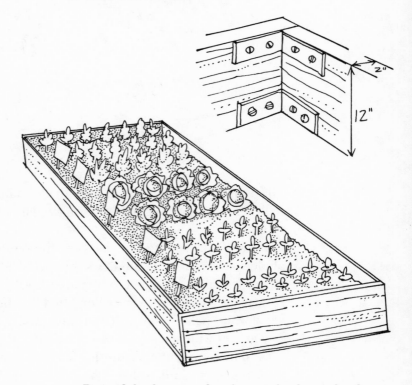

Raised beds can also be made from the large
planter boxes available at garden supply houses. If
these are used on a balcony, try putting ball-bearing casters on them so they can be moved about to

take advantage of the sun. A concrete balcony or asphalt-covered roof reflects a great deal of heat in mid-summer. It would be wise to place some sort of dark, light-absorbing plastic or other weatherproof material beneath the planter. Indoor-outdoor carpeting is a good heat absorber and remnants are easy to find in rug or department stores.

If the container on hand is not as decorative as you might like, then look for a container for the container. A coffee can inside a wicker basket works fine (line the bottom of the basket with sphagnum moss which is available at garden supply shops and most variety stores). Nail kegs (about 14-inch diameter, 20-inches high) are frequently available at garden shops, hardware stores, and lumber yards for $3 to $5. Bushel baskets have also made a comeback and are easier to find in both city and suburb than they were a few years ago. They offer another planting possibility.

Any kind of plastic bag—freezer, bread, grocery produce, garbage can liner—can make an inexpensive and highly successful container. Plants can remain in the bags from seeding to harvest-time. Fill them with a soil mix (see page 26), leaving enough room so that the top of the bag can be fastened with a "twist-um" or folded flat and stapled shut. Place each bag long-side down, flatten out the soil, punch holes where the seeds are to go and others in the bottom for drainage. Then place the plastic "soil pillows" in some other container to collect run-off when the plants are watered. Your choice of an outer container is nearly limitless since the pillow can be molded to fit any shape or size planter.

Would-be gardeners with absolutely no outdoor space needn't despair. You do have windows. An entire window area can be expanded into a bay-type greenhouse if you own your apartment or townhouse, say, or if you have a cooperative landlord. These window greenhouse units can be purchased commercially, custom prefabricated to fit the space, and can be installed from the inside.

An average window can accommodate a greenhouse that will provide 15 to 20 square feet of growing area. (Local ordinance might prohibit such overhang; tenants should check this out before placing any orders.) There are also tiny windowsill greenhouses ranging in price from $5 to $50, which will house small plants. And, of course, there is always the windowsill itself—usually large enough for a pot or two. If not, windowsill extenders are available through catalogues, or you can widen the sill yourself simply with the addition of shelving supported by brackets.

To supplement the sills still further, add hanging baskets, indoors or out. What could be nicer for Tiny Tim cherry tomatoes. Wire baskets are quite satisfactory and very reasonable—$1 or $2. French wire baskets, those such as salad greens are washed in, are practical and decorative. Bicycle baskets (sans bicycle) can also be planted. Line wire baskets with unmilled sphagnum moss which has been thoroughly soaked in water. Pack the wet moss

in the basket, lining the bottom and sides with at least an inch-and-a-half thickness of moss. Then add potting soil and the plant. Cover the top soil with another layer of moss, which will help the basket retain moisture longer.

Other kinds of pots can also be hung. Holes can be drilled for chains in wooden ones; ceramic pots can be suspended in a rope cradle. If you are into macramé, both simple and elaborate hangings can be designed, and in colors to suit yourself.

The containers, as well as their crops, will do much to brighten the decor of a balcony, patio or doorstep, as well as the rooms of your home. You can go op, mod, traditional—whatever your fancy. But do, always, let the plants take center stage. You will find that plain clay pots, pails and stone jars are far more practical (and easier to live with) than the philodendron-in-a-coffee-grinder type of planter.

Take a tour of the dime or hardware store. The housewares department is a good place to find inexpensive containers, often of excellent design. Look for bowls, tubs and baskets; for kettles, pots and pans; for boxes and buckets. How about a colander for something a bit offbeat but not too "cute"? Lined with plastic vinyl, with a few holes repunched in the bottom, and filled with a layer of

gravel, the soil and a planting of parsley, it will be charming and practical—unpretentious and perfectly suited for its use.

Clay, wood, pottery, plastic, metal, Styrofoam —almost anything can be used for plants provided it has adequate holes for drainage. The main distinctions between different type containers are in their drainage provisions and porosity of the container material. These two factors mainly determine the amount and frequency of watering needed. For plants to obtain both air and water—which they must have to survive—the roots must be alternately dry and wet. Extremes of either, of course, affect the health of the plants adversely.

Make sure the container you choose has adequate drainage. If it is less than 10 inches in diameter, one ½-inch diameter hole is enough. Containers over 10 inches in diameter—other than clay pots which are quite porous—should have three or four ½-inch holes. If the container is porous, air and water can enter through it and less drainage provision is required. The following paragraphs summarize the qualities of porosity and drainage of various types of containers.

Ordinary Clay Pot—*Clay is porous, allowing air and water to pass through the sides of the pot and the soil inside; existing drainage holes are adequate in size and number.*

Wooden Container—*Less porous than clay; often comes without a drainage hole in the bottom, in which case holes may be drilled; otherwise, a two-inch layer of coarse gravel or perlite should be placed in the bottom before adding soil.*

Plastic Container—*Not at all porous. Less frequent watering is needed, which can be an advantage if you are often away for weekends.*

Styrofoam Pots—*Air porous but not water porous; less frequent watering is required than with clay pots.*

Plastic Bags—*Neither air nor water porous; since there is practically no evaporation from a sealed plastic container, less frequent watering required.*

Raised Bed—*Because of its large surface area, porosity of the container material is less of a factor than with pots and smaller containers. For good drainage and air circulation, place a two-inch layer of coarse gravel in the bottom before adding soil; or use a two-inch layer of a light porous stone called featherock (available at lumber yards) if weight is a critical factor, as it is likely to be on roofs. Styrofoam packing materials or even old Styrofoam coolers crumbled to peanut-sized pieces can also be used for drainage provision. There is a high rate of evaporation in raised beds and daily watering is essential.*

Hanging Baskets—*A basket dries out very quickly and will likely require daily watering. It should be hung where it can be easily retrieved for watering, which is best done by submerging the basket up to the soil level in a container of water and letting it soak for a few minutes. Remove and let it drain for a few minutes longer before changing. Usually, no provision is made to catch drainage, which could be a distraction if the basket overhangs a walkway.*

Hanging Pots—*Usually there is an attached saucer to catch drainage water, but even so, hanging pots dry out rather quickly and require daily watering. In planting hanging baskets and pots, leave an inch or so between the top of the soil and the rim of the container. Otherwise, in watering, the water will be over the side of the container before it soaks through.*

As your farm expands, and it will, you may find that grouping the containers on a tea cart, a kitchen utility cart, a child's wagon, a wheelbarrow or a heavy piece of plywood (three-quarter inch, exterior grade) with ball-bearing casters attached will make the job of caring for your crops easier. On chilly nights in early spring and fall, or when there is inclement weather, such as hail or high winds, you'll be able to move the plants to a more protected place—to a sheltered corner or indoors, if need be. Come bad weather, you'll be thankful that you can roll your garden to safety and not have to depend on a hastily rigged plastic shield that may quickly be blown to shreds.

One further word on gardening space. Many apartment buildings have outside fire escapes, which may appear to be just the spot for a pot or planter. However, the ordinances of most cities prohibit, and the National Fire Prevention Authority urges, that no container of any kind be placed on fire escapes. Some local prevention authorities allow baskets or planters to be hung from a fire escape if they do not interfere with egress from the building. Check with your local fire prevention authority first.

2. Improving on the Good Earth

To get started, you really don't need much more than a pot, some dirt and a seed to put in it. But while getting the container is relatively simple, putting your hands in some dirt can be something of a problem. Sometimes, the only real dirt an urbanite encounters (other than the airborne variety) is that owned by the city in its public parks—and officials frown on citizens carrying it home in flowerpots. So, if you must be a real dirt gardener, persuade a suburban or farmer friend to part with some topsoil, rather than resorting to furtive trips at dusk with your son's pail and shovel.

Real dirt is fine for plants safely past sprouting and seedling stage and ready for transplant. Or for use with rootstock of dwarf citrus and other fruit trees. (To lighten its weight and texture, mix in some artificial soil.) But beware. Even the best of garden soils should be sterilized before being used for seeds.

Probably the greatest danger in the use of unsterilized soil is the likelihood of a fungus disease carried in the spores of the soil. Called "damping off," this affliction is a depressing and discouraging experience. The seeds sprout, vigorous plants emerge and then, quite suddenly, the stems shrink and shrivel just above the soil level. Those little plants that once held such bright promise collapse and die almost overnight.

To avoid "damping off" and other equally disastrous though perhaps less dramatic "happenings," you must sterilize the honest-to-goodness-kind of dirt before you use it for potting soil in which to plant seeds. The usual home method is to bake it in the oven in a flat pan, for at least one hour, at 215°. However, before you decide to test your culinary skill, let us say that it is not as simple a job as all that. It can, in fact, make an awful mess—and a worse smell. Moreover, you should wait at least two weeks before using the soil. The waiting period allows the ammonia released in the heating process to escape.

For these reasons, most container gardeners find it expedient, for the limited amount of gardening they do, to buy a commercially prepared growing medium (variously referred to as artificial or synthetic or formula potting soils); or to buy the readily available ingredients that they can mix themselves.

The packaged artificial soils have many advantages: they are specially formulated to provide a good growing medium for your plants; they are free from disease organisms, nematodes (a root-attacking pest) and weed seed; and they are much lighter than ordinary soil, making it much easier to move the container about, if need be. Where an eight-inch plastic pot containing regular soil might weigh about 10 pounds, the same pot filled with artficial soil would weigh only about four and one-half pounds. The texture is also light and porous, allowing root crops to develop well and water to drain properly.

Artificial soils are available in various package sizes, ranging from as small an amount as a quart and costing under a dollar up to a 2½-bushel bag costing about $12. A bushel will provide enough soil for 25 one-gallon containers. Some soil mixes include nutrients to nourish the plants for several weeks; others need to have nutrients added as soon as the seeds sprout. Potting mix designed for African violets is not suitable for vegetables, as its texture is too fine.

For those who wish to mix their own soil, the following "recipe" will make seven or eight bushels—enough to launch an ambitious gardening venture or to divide with neighbors and friends. The ingredients are available in garden stores in the approximate sizes listed (with the exception of limestone) and in smaller sizes as well, for those whose requirements are less.

One four-cubic-foot bag of sphagnum moss

One four-cubic-foot bag of vermiculite

Two and one-half pounds of limestone. (About the smallest pre-packaged bag you can buy is 10 pounds but limestone is inexpensive—under a dollar a bag.)

and either

Two pounds of a tomato food type fertilizer, a 6-18-6 or 5-10-10 formula, for example. (See A Balanced Diet, page 44, to unravel the mystery of these numbers, which aren't really as confusing as they seem.)

or

Two pounds of 5-10-5 fertilizer plus one pound of superphosphate (0-20-0)

Pour all of these ingredients together in a pile on a piece of canvas or heavy plastic (press the shower curtain into service if nothing else is available). The balcony, porch or, as a last resort, the kitchen or bathroom is your work area. Use hot water to moisten the ingredients as you add each one to the pile. The water cuts down on the dust, and if it is hot, the moss absorbs it better.

Don't try to stir the mixture to blend it; it's too much of a job. Instead, lift it by shovelfuls. Use a sturdy dustpan if you don't have the right tool on hand (and it's hard to imagine you will if you live in an apartment). You'll find the mixing a bit hard on the back, but carry on through the pile, picking up a little of each ingredient and then putting it down in another spot to form a new pile. Repeat the whole process to put the pile back where it was before. If you are stirring up more dust than your nose can stand, sprinkle on a little more water. Move the pile one more time, and you should have it well mixed. And now that you know the procedure for mixing your own you may well decide to buy the stuff already packaged.

3. Selecting and Sowing Seed

Individual packages of vegetable seed are displayed on racks not only in garden and nursery centers, but in grocery, variety and hardware stores. The selections usually include one or two varieties of the most commonly grown vegetables. If your seed buying will be limited to an item or two—a packet of radishes and one of lettuce, for example—it makes sense to buy from the rack. (When you do, check to see that the date stamped on the packet is for the current planting year. The date is your guarantee that the seed you buy is fresh and viable.)

However, for more ambitious gardening than the seed rack offers (and why not?) do your shopping through the seed catalogues, too. Write to one or two seed houses (names and addresses of a number of seed companies are listed on page 112). Catalogues are usually prepared for distribution around December or January, so you can shop at your leisure, make selections, order and have the plant material delivered to you in plenty of time for spring, or pre-spring planting.

Within the last few years, many fruit and vegetable varieties have been developed especially for container gardening, or for the gardener with a pocket-sized piece of land. There are now dwarf and miniature fruits and vegetables of almost every kind—peach, cucumber, lima bean, even corn. Without a catalogue to browse through, you'll miss out on the wide selection of potential crops, and the new and improved varieties for container gardening that come along each year. The catalogues are also fascinating to read and the true farmer—whether he measures his land by the acre or the inch— always saves a few winter evenings for these informative and colorful publications.

Seeds for some crops can be sown directly into the containers in which they will mature while other crops are started with two or three seeds in small individual pots or in "flats." After these plants reach seedling stage, they are then "potted up" (transferred to a larger container). Consult the instructions pertaining to individual crops at the end of this book and also the seed packet instructions to determine whether to plant directly into permanent containers or to sow first in smaller pots.

If the crop dictates planting small first, your initial sowing can be in most any container on hand, although a fairly large shallow box two to three inches deep (called a flat) accommodates more seeds and is easier to handle than a deep pot. An oblong cake pan would be fine. If it's your best or one-and-only, line it with plastic to prevent discoloration. The deeper foil pans that frozen foods come in make good flats, too.

Some provision must be made for drainage, however. Although it is desirable to have drainage holes in the bottom, it is not absolutely necessary. A one-half-inch layer of perlite or small-size gravel in the bottom will effect satisfactory drainage. Add a level layer of potting soil an inch and one-half or two inches deep, moisten the soil and let it settle a bit. Now sow the seeds on the surface, spacing them according to seed packet instructions. (Directions for spacing and planting depth are always given on the back of seed packets.) Cover the seeds with the appropriate amount of damp potting soil. Firm the soil in place—tamping it lightly with the bottom of a water glass or with your hand.

For no other reason than that once in a great while a seed fails to germinate, sow about twice the number of seeds than the number of plants desired. You will, no doubt, have many more seeds than you need in each packet. Don't go overboard, though, and plant them all. Any left-overs can be kept for another year. Just store them in a cool airy place; as long as they have air but no moisture, they will continue to "live" but be dormant. (Put the packets in a small jar, punch a couple of holes in the lid, and store them in the refrigerator on a bottom shelf, away from the ice compartment.)

After the seeds are planted, cover the entire flat with clear plastic film but don't let it touch the seedbed. The film will help provide a properly humid atmosphere for seed growth. You will not need to add additional water until the seeds have sprouted. As a matter of fact, check every few days to make certain that the soil is not too moist or mildew will begin to grow. If it appears, remove the film and put the flat in full sun for a few hours so that the soil will dry out promptly. Best practice, of course, is not to use too much water to begin with—only enough to moisten the soil. Place the flat in a warm place (65 to 75 degrees) though not in the sun, nor near direct heat.

Now begins that breathless period of waiting for the first bit of green. The time required for germination (beginning of growth) varies with the individual plants; the seed packet almost always provides this information. Most seeds seem to germinate more quickly in the dark, though a few prefer the light. If the seed packet does not state the plant's preference, gamble on the dark. Placing a newspaper over the top of the plastic-covered flat for the germination period specified on the seed packet is a good idea—although you'll probably find yourself peeking several times a day "to see if they've come up yet." When they do, the first thing to appear will be a tender, sometimes fat, sometimes thin, white loop as the stem of the plant begins to lift itself from the soil.

Now, remove the newspaper and the plastic film and give the flat full light but NO direct sun. In another day, the stems will be up nicely, possibly a half inch tall. By now, you may need to add water to keep the soil slightly moist; do so lightly with a sprinkler-type watering can or a clothes sprinkler. (Water poured on directly in a heavy stream displaces the light-weight soil and can disturb the plants' growth.)

In another day or so, the first leaves will unfold.

These are called the "heart leaves"; they are followed in three or four days by two more leaves. These are called "true leaves," distinguished from the heart leaves in that their shape and texture is representative of the mature plant foliage. At this stage, the plants are called seedlings.

Because you sowed more seeds than the number of plants you really want or have room for, you now must thin out the surplus seedlings. This should be done when the seedlings are large enough for their leaves to touch their neighbors (except for lettuce and several other salad greens). However heartless this task seems, it's basic to good farming. If you are to provide your seedlings with the best opportunity for growth, you must ruthlessly eliminate any

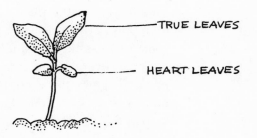

SEEDLING

TRUE LEAVES

HEART LEAVES

THINNING WITH SCISSORS
AT SOIL LINE

excess competition for your plants' food, water and growing room.

The best tool for thinning seedlings is a pair of thin, sharp scissors (manicure, seamstress, or barber shears work fine) to reach between the plants and snip off each unnecessary seedling at the soil line. Do not thin by pulling the seedlings out by their heads, for no matter how tiny they are, their removal can disturb the root system of the plants that are to remain.

And don't try to save extra seedlings for transplant. In the first place, you already have all the plants you can handle but, more important, transplanted or weeded-out seedlings have a high percentage of failures. It is usually far better just to dispose of the surplus.

When the seedlings have four or six true leaves (two or three pairs) or are beginning to crowd each other, it is time to transplant them into a larger container. This process almost necessarily involves disturbing the roots of the plant. Your objective is to accomplish the transplanting with as little shock to them as possible. So have the individual containers in which you want the young plants to continue growth all ready before you touch a leaf.

The containers should, of course, be clean. Then, place a piece of mesh screen or a shard (piece of broken clay pot, the curved side facing down so that the water drains under and out) in the bottom of the container to cover the drainage holes; this will allow the water to run out but will keep the next layer of gravel from plugging up the hole or the soil from coming out. Next, add about a half-inch to an inch of perlite, gravel, or pebbles. Actually, anything that is non-decayable and non-packing will do—marbles, bottle caps, broken bits of pottery, or those white plastic peanuts used widely as packing material. Finally, begin to add the soil mix, up to about two-thirds full. This is the stage at which you can put to use regular garden dirt.

Have the flat slightly damp, so that when the young plants are separated and lifted out, at least some soil will cling to their roots. Use an old kitchen fork to break the soil about an inch or so away from and all around the young plant. Then with a lifting, wedging action, gently lift the plant up and out of the soil and, handling it by the leaves (so as not to bruise the tender stem), place it immediately into the prepared container. If the flat is a frozen food pan, it can be cut apart with an old pair of scissors and the plants lifted out with a spatula. Don't worry too much about setting the plant at the proper depth. With the exception of strawberries and trees, this is not a critical factor for most plants. Most vegetable crops should be set a little deeper in the permanent location than they were in the seedbed, and tomatoes profit by being set with half of the stem below the soil line.

Now add more potting soil up to an inch or so of the top of the container. Firm the soil with your hands—firming down into the pot, rather than around the stem of the plant. Then set the entire container into a larger one to soak up water, or else water with a sprinkler-type can from above. Either way, as moisture enters, the soil will settle, possibly a half-inch. Add enough additional soil to bring the level back to within an inch or so of the top.

A much more convenient route from seed to seedling stage, and one that avoids all the bother of transplanting, is through the use of individual seedling peat pots. These are simply small pots made of compressed peat moss; sometimes, 75 percent compressed peat moss and 25 percent compressed wood fiber. You fill the peat pot with soil mix, then plant two or three seeds to a pot. (Later you will thin to one seedling per pot.)

When the seedlings reach transplant stage, soak the peat pot and cut away the bottom of it. Then put the seedling with its peat pot band around it into the soil in your larger or permanent container. The plant roots will have ready access to the new soil from the bottom while the peat pot band will gradu-

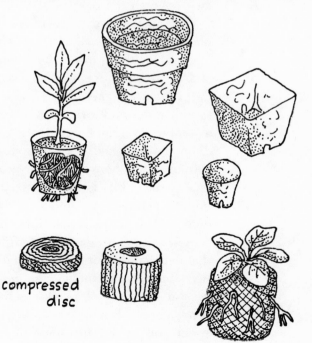

compressed
disc

ally disintegrate, nurturing the plant in the process. Peat pots are available at garden supply houses and in many variety stores at 3¢ to 25¢ each, depending on the number, size and kind you buy. They range in size from one and one-half to four inches in diameter. Another type of peat pot comes as a compressed disc, which when soaked in water, expands into a small, one-inch pot complete with planting medium (soil mix) and plant nutrients; all you do is add the seed.

Cardboard egg containers are also good for sowing seed. Each half provides a separate "pot" for 12 plants. The carton may be cut apart and each "pot" transplanted to its permanent container. The pressed cardboard bottom of the carton should be cut away as with the peat pot.

Still another way to start seeds is to use preplanted containers. Usually plastic, these containers contain the growing medium, initial nutrients and the seeds already in place. You merely take the container home, punch holes in the clear plastic lid, water and wait. A number of vegetables are available in this type planter at grocery, drug, dime, novelty and hardware stores as well as in garden supply houses and nurseries. The disadvantage of these kits is that the seedlings will have to be transplanted later into separate containers. The choice of varieties is also limited.

A separate pot for each seedling, especially one that decomposes after it is planted, repays the extra investment many times over, not only in the successful handling of plants, but also in time and convenience. But whether you go the "flat" or the "peat pot" route, the important thing is that the plant's growth not be interrupted. Once you plant seeds and get the plant started, growth should proceed steadily. Time lost in transplanting plus the shock to the plant's system will take their toll.

One further caution. After one or two unseasonably mild days in February or March, all gardeners are hard to restrain. The city farmer is no exception and must be especially patient. If seeds are sown too early, the plants will reach transplant stage and be ready for the great outdoors well before the weatherman allows. Plants at this stage will not continue to thrive as they should if they have to remain indoors. Therefore, do not sow the seeds any sooner than six to eight weeks before they can be safely moved outdoors. Call your local National Weather Service station (listed in the phone book under the U.S. Government, Department of Commerce) and ask them for the last predicted frost date in your area. After this date, plants can be safely moved outdoors. Put the seedlings out for an hour or two the first day (in a shaded area) and gradually increase the period of exposure so that by the end of a week they have grown accustomed to the temperature change and the more direct rays of the sun. This process of acclimation is called "hardening." If the sunlight is very intense you should rig up a device to shade the seedlings. Suggestions for sunshades are discussed in the next chapter.

4. Shedding Light on the Subject

Once you begin to farm—whether on your balcony, patio, windowsill or roof—you will become acutely sensitive to changes in the sun's position in the sky as the summer progresses. What was a bright spot on the balcony in May, may not be so in August, or vice versa. Before deciding definitely on what crops to grow, consider rather carefully the amount of sunlight available for the plants. If your "farm" faces east, there will be morning sunlight, but the spot will be shaded from the afternoon sun by your building. If you are on the north side, you will probably receive only morning sun, depending somewhat on the time of the year. A southern exposure will receive both early morning and late afternoon sun. On the west, of course, you will have no morning sunlight, but will enjoy the long afternoon and twilight rays. Probably the only city garden to receive full sun throughout the day would be a roof or penthouse terrace.

Many crops need full sun but there are a number of others that can get along with part sun, part shade. To provide their plants with the best possible environment, city farmers can move them about, following the sun's rays as the crops and seasons dictate. The more portable the containers, the greater the flexibility.

Light is a form of energy and some crops need more of it than others. Heading the list are plants that produce fruit—not only peaches or figs, but also eggplant and green pepper. Root crops, such as radishes and carrots, can get along with less light. Leaf crops, such as lettuce and chard, are the least demanding.

If the amount of sunlight available to the garden is severely limited, you might consider using supplemental light. Scientists have developed fluorescent lamps for indoor use that provide energy in the form that plants can absorb—light rays in the red and blue spectrum. These fluorescent lamps give off a soft, cool light. Regular incandescent lamps can and do produce energy, but most of it (about 80 percent) is in the form of heat rather than light; the light they emit—in the yellow and green color spectrum—is usually not required by vegetable plants until the blossoming stage.

High-intensity fluorescent lamps are of distinct benefit in starting seedlings, which can use as much as 18 hours of light per day. (It is easy to determine when seedlings are not receiving enough light—the plants will grow tall and spindly, stretching their stems toward the light source.)

High-output grow lamps are described in some seed catalogues and are also available at garden and hardware stores. (Two of these are known commercially as Gro-Lux and Agro-Lite.) If you have an ordinary fluorescent lamp, it can also be used.

If you do plan to try supplemental lighting, check the catalogue to see what is available. There is a wide range of lamps from simple, fluorescent tubes at $3.50 to use in your own fixture, to multiple-tube, multi-plant tray stands that cost as much as $225, with, fortunately, a number of choices in between. Some fixtures combine fluorescent and incandescent light. Read the descriptions carefully to decide which will best suit your needs.

It is probably wise at the beginning to think small. Experiment at first with growing seedlings under a single small unit. The results will probably be so pleasing—sturdy, compact plants—that you will want to go on to more elaborate fixtures as your living space allows. Keep in mind that houseplants can also be grown along with your crops (and should be, for the fetching combinations and color they can add to a plant grouping), and many do splendidly under lights. Gardening under lights is, in fact, a fast-growing hobby in itself.

Remember, however, that even the best supplemental light has its limits. For example, grow lamps would not be practical as the main source of light for bringing tomatoes into fruit, for they simply do not come anywhere near to delivering the equivalent energy of the sun. On the other hand, artificial light can be used successfully to establish the sturdiest, healthiest seedlings you have ever seen, to produce leaf crops, to keep an herb garden thriving or to give a boost to or lengthen the daylight time of other crops.

The container gardener who has full sunlight available may have his problems, too. Full sunlight can be a mixed blessing for crops on a patio, balcony or other spot where the reflection from brick, concrete and paving can produce intense heat. Cool-season crops—lettuce or radishes, for example—are not heat-hardy and will not survive such a situation. An eggplant or tomato is more heat-tolerant and will thrive if cared for properly and protected from intense heat.

Various arrangements can be devised to protect plants during the hottest part of the midsummer days. One way to conquer the sun is to cut out a number of one-inch strips from an inexpensive beach umbrella, thus creating a slatted sunshade over the plants. Heat-absorbing materials placed under and in back of plants can also help cut down on reflected heat. For roof gardens, protection can be inexpensively contrived with bamboo shades, awnings or a sheet of Plexiglas or fiberglass.

For the cool-season plants, simply start them early enough to beat the heat. Have them safely raised and eaten before the dog days of summer arrive. (The Growth Chart on page 109 indicates the preferred growing season for various vegetables.)

5. Serving a Balanced Diet

Plants need a balanced diet just as people do, and you will find that they are heavy feeders. However, though they like to be fed before they get too hungry, they do not like to be stuffed. A steady supply of essential nutrients is what is needed to keep them thriving.

The three main elements in a plant's diet are nitrogen, phosphorus and potassium. The numbers which identify fertilizer formulas—whether 20-10-4, 4-10-6, 5-10-5 or any of the many other combinations—refer to the percentage of these three elements in the formula. The number are always given in this order: the percentage of nitrogen first, phosphorus second and potassium third.

Different plants require different amounts of these elements and the same plant's needs also vary depending upon the stage of its development. Nitrogen, for example, is believed to be most important when a plant is growing fast and producing foliage. When the plant is flowering and setting fruit, it needs phosphorus. Potassium is necessary for strong, healthy roots.

In the most general terms, leafy vegetables—lettuce, spinach, chard—prefer nitrogen for making tender, juicy leaves. Fruit-bearing crops—tomato, eggplant, green peppers—respond to phosphorus. Root crops—radishes, carrots, beets—like potassium.

Various trace elements are also important in a plant's diet and the one most often lacking is iron. You may note from time to time that the leaves on your plants are yellowing while the veins remain green. The condition is likely to be chlorosis and can be corrected by the addition of chelated iron to the plant's diet.

Don't let all the hocus-pocus that seems to surround the fertilizer "mystique" unduly alarm you. It does not require deep scientific study. You can, in fact, simply buy plant foods that are formulated specifically for the types of plants you wish to grow. Tomato food, for example, will be packaged and labeled as such. It is high in phosphorus and is effective for a number of other crops, as the label will point out. As a matter of fact, if you are to choose just one fertilizer to use, pick one with a proportionately high middle number (for phosphorus) in relation to the other two.

You will find fertilizer packaged in sizes as small as eight ounces. Some fertilizers are to be dissolved in water (one teaspoon or one tablespoon to a gallon of water, for example) and then applied to the plant. Such soluble foods are quickly available to the plant. Other fertilizers come in tablet or pellet form to be pressed into the soil not too close to the plant. These release their nutrients more slowly and over a longer period of time.

When you transplant seedlings, give them a fertilizer treatment and regular feedings thereafter. There are no specific rules for the amount to use or the frequency of application, but a good general guide is to resist the reasoning, "If a little is good, a lot is better." It's just not so. Nitrogen, for example, produces results you can see—and fast! Foliage greens up and grows quickly. The temptation is great to give the plant more than it actually needs or is good for it. Too much nitrogen encourages foliage growth at the expense of flowers and fruit. Unusually dark green, brittle foliage and weak stems are fairly accurate indications of nitrogen over-feeding. Best follow package directions to the letter. These instructions have been worked out carefully to ensure the best performance from the products.

If you have a blender you can use it to whip up an extra taste treat for your container plants. Put in vegetable peelings, lettuce leaves, egg shells and whatever other attractive garbage you may have on hand. Add water (enough to wind up with a very thin liquid) and then give the whole business a good whirl in the blender. (Most of these mixtures will look awful.)

You can add this health-food treatment to your plants once every couple of weeks in place of plain watering. The minerals are not only good for your plants but in the recycling of at least some organic materials in your gardening venture you can help ease any vaguely sinful feelings you may have about being dependent upon chemical fertilizers.

If you have even a small piece of Mother Earth to garden in—a window box even—then kitchen garbage belongs in your garden on a routine basis. Start as soon as space becomes available after harvest in the fall. Chop the kitchen scraps up fine, dig a hole in the garden, dump the chopped mixture in, add a bit of fertilizer, cover back up with dirt and water well. Pick a new spot each time and by frost you'll have a good underlayer of organic matter which, come spring, you can turn up and mix through the soil.

6. Providing for Adequate Water

The novice soon learns—mostly by experience, not reading books—how much water to give his plants. Use your eyes (Does the soil *look* dry? Do the leaves *look* limp?) and also your touch (Does the soil *feel* dry? Do the leaves *feel* parched?) . Crops grown in containers dry out quickly from sun and wind, and the smaller the planter, the faster the soil will lose water. Check the containers each day. The soil should not be constantly soggy, but neither should it dry out completely. It should feel slightly moist to the touch. With only a little experience, you'll get the "feel" of it.

You can also learn to judge water content by the weight of the container (if they are small enough to lift comfortably). A container will seem relatively light when the plant needs water. If the container is too large to lift, give it a sharp tap with your knuckles. If there is a hollow, ringing sound, the plant needs water; if there is a dull thump, wait a while.

If plants are outdoors, they will almost surely need daily watering. Give enough water so that it reaches the bottom of the pot and drains through. See that the pots have adequate drainage (drainage hole and layer of perlite, gravel or pebbles) so excess water won't settle around the roots. Keep a saucer (clay, pottery, soup or cereal bowl or pie tin) under the smaller containers. After about 10 to 15 minutes, the container can be lifted and the saucer emptied. This will keep the plant from having "wet feet."

For larger containers, or a group of smaller containers, place the pots on a shallow tray that has been filled with pebbles. A shallow roasting pan works fine. (Teflon-coated pans are generally more attractive than those of shiny aluminum.) Excess water drains off into the pebbles while the container remains above water level. Indoors, this practice also adds extra moisture to the air, a boon to plants relegated to the dry atmosphere of most apartments.

In the city, there's also the problem of soot and other airborne dirt accumulating on your plants (and clogging their pores) unless they are kept wiped clean. Lightly dusting the leaves with a dry cloth rather than a damp one may work better because some of this gunk is greasy and has a tendency to smear when wet. Pouring water over the plant doesn't work too well, because it takes a good bit of water (as well as care in where and how you splash it) and the method is generally inefficient and messy.

If the stuff that settles on your plants is oily and

sticks to the leaves, then use a warm, slightly soapy cloth to give the plant leaves an occasional bath. Follow up with a rinse with a damp cloth or put them in the shower if you can adjust the showerhead for a fine mist. If the kitchen or bathroom faucets are close enough, you can rig up an efficient watering and bathing system for your crops by using a separate shower head attached to rubber tubing fitted onto the regular faucet. Trail the tubing through a window if you have to, to reach the porch or balcony. Such a portable watering system will save many a step.

If your plants begin to show signs of a too dry atmosphere as evidenced by yellowing foliage or leaf drop, they will benefit greatly from misting. Little hand misters are sold in garden or discount stores. If you still have baby's vaporizer on hand, this is an excellent way to increase the humidity of your indoor garden. Use it with just plain water, of course.

7. Tender Loving Care

Surely no one who troubles to sow a seed needs to be told that TLC is a built-in part of successful gardening, but for city farmers such commitment is crucial. There's no need to tiptoe in, at 2 A.M., to see if your seedlings are still breathing, nor must you panic at first sight of a faintly yellow leaf and rush to administer five or six different life-saving remedies at once. Tender loving care means dependability: that you check on your plants every day; that you water and feed them when necessary; that you provide for their care when you must be away (even one day on a hot roof in midsummer without water could be catastrophic). You must also shelter your plants from wind and storms and searing sun, and wipe their leaves or give them baths when needed.

Keep in mind, too, the limits of your land, and don't over-populate the plot. City farmers are often guilty of over-enthusiasm. One look at a catalogue's tempting pictures and glowing descriptions and the call of the earth gets totally out of hand. Tomatoes, peppers, lettuce and radishes won't seem enough. So why not some eggplant? The beets look easy. Carrots take no space at all. Here's a spinach that can grow against the wall!

Such euphoria is common to almost all city gardeners when they first discover that they can grow fruits and vegetables as well as African violets. And that's part of the fun. But the available amount of space and sunlight, as well as the size of your pocketbook, are practical realities. While enjoying the catalogue, think of the number of containers involved, the pounds (perhaps tons) of soil to be moved and hours of care that your plants will require.

Farm whatever space you have, but don't go beyond what it and you can reasonably produce. Resist the temptation to plant too many seeds of the same crop (unless you plan to give away the extra seedlings—and they do make nice gifts). And be careful not to plant too many kinds of crops in any one year. One fruit-laden tomato plant, a thriving green pepper and a mint-condition container or two of lettuce and radishes are far more rewarding than ten assorted pots of this and that, all in various stages of anemia and struggling for survival. After all, there's always another spring.

So, be selective—think big but start small. Try anything that tempts your palate. The nicest part of gardening is that you can become an "expert" in the time it takes to bring a plant from seed to the supper table.

WHAT CAN
YOU GROW?

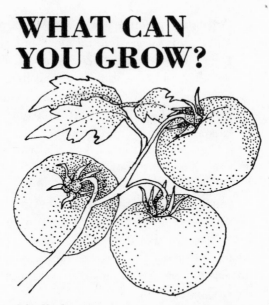

Tomatoes Of all the grow-your-own crops, tomatoes are the most rewarding. For the space they take, they pay handsome dividends not only in the amount of fruit produced (continuously over a long season) but in quality. Vine-ripened fruits make the market offering seem unpalatable. Wait till you taste your first home-grown crop.

Since seedlings of the tomato varieties best suited for container gardening are not widely available in local stores, plan on starting plants from seed. Shop the catalogues and get an order in early enough so that the seeds can be started at least six to eight weeks in advance of the last predicted frost. (The seed packet will sometimes give outdoor planting dates by geographic zones. If it doesn't, call the local Weather Service for your area's average frost free date.) Find the date for the zone in which you live, then count back eight weeks to determine when to sow seeds indoors. For best re-sults, sow in individual peat pots and transplant later to permanent containers. Wait until the weather is dependably warm before putting the seedlings out. Remember to accustom them gradu-ally to outdoor living, particularly if they have been raised under artificial light.

Pre-planted tomato kits are available from some seed houses. Small cubes of artificial soil enclosed in thin clear plastic film contain the necessary nutrients—and the seeds. Just add water and the miniature greenhouse will produce seedlings for transplant. For the city grower who can share with a friend or two, this is an inexpensive and effortless way to grow seedings—the cost of 20 cubes being a little more than $2.

Most tomato plants will need to be staked; even the miniatures benefit from a small stake to provide support when the plant reaches full size and is bearing fruit. Insert the stake in the soil about two inches from the stem at the same time the plant is moved to its permanent container. Otherwise you may disturb or damage the roots. You can also use a trellis or railing for support or, with the larger plants, even try espalier (training them horizontally against an upright flat surface). When tying plants to stakes and railings, use strips of soft cloth rags or old nylon stockings—string or cord will cut into the stalk.

Tomatoes need warm temperatures to mature and produce. See that they have full sun, but protect them from scorching heat and wind. Plants in con-tainers also require a great deal of water throughout their bearing season.

Steady, continuous growth is the key to delicious and abundant fruit, so make sure that the plants have adequate food. Fertilize the seedlings at transplanting time, again in three weeks and about once a week while they are producing fruit. Buy one of the fertilizers specially formulated for tomatoes. They provide the proper amount of phosphorus needed for setting fruit without too much nitrogen that would cause most of the plant's growth to go to vine.

Tomatoes raised on a windowsill or in a sheltered location may need a substitute for the bees and breeze to accomplish pollination. Otherwise, the plants may bloom prolifically but set no fruit. Each day while the plants are in blossom, give them a gentle shake to distribute the pollen. And remember that new blossoms will be opening each day over quite a long period of time.

Extremes in temperature may also cause blossoms to drop without setting fruit. Watch out for night temperatures below 55 degrees and above 68 degrees and day temperatures above 95 degrees. Make sure to move the plants to shelter on cold nights and to shade them on very hot days.

Hormone-type sprays can also be used to help the blossoms from falling before they set fruit. These sprays, available in aerosols that produce a fine mist, are effective when blossoms drop due to cold nights. They will not help when blossom drop is due to high temperature.

As the plants grow, you will want to prune them somewhat, to the extent of taking off the first two or three "suckers" as they form. Suckers are the little shoots that appear between the main stem and the

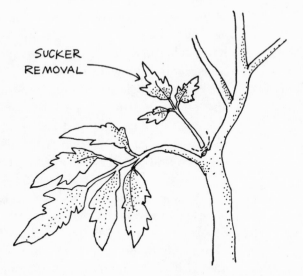

SUCKER
REMOVAL

branches. Pinch or snip them out. There are different schools of thought on tomato pruning—one says that tomatoes are better off pruned to a single main stem; another maintains that it is best to let the plant develop several stems.

The city farmer must consider the particular environment his plants will have. If they are to be in full sun, on a patio or terrace, say, where reflected heat is also a factor, it may be better not to prune the plants, at least not any more than the first two or three suckers. The other suckers can then form secondary stems and the extra foliage will provide more shade for the fruit. On the other hand, if the plant will not be exposed to direct, searing sunlight, then pruning to a single stem by removing all the suckers as they appear will open up the plant to more light. (If you have more than one pot of tomatoes, don't crowd them together.)

Depending on the variety, you may expect your

first tomato about 50 to 80 days after planting the seeds. With proper care (light, water, food, air), the vines will continue to produce right through the fall. If the plants still have green tomatoes on them when frost threatens, bring them indoors. The tomatoes will ripen on the vine inside, even though the plant itself may have yellowed and withered leaves.

If the vines are a bit too scraggly to be passed off as potted plants, pull them up by the roots and if you can find a cool out-of-the-way place, hang them upside down over a line; the fruit will ripen from the energy and moisture stored in the vine. A basement is a good place—light is not especially required; an apartment storage room would work, if not too close to the furnace, or they can even be strung up in a cool part of the apartment, if you don't mind visitors' stares.

The choice of varieties for container gardening includes miniature plants that produce miniature fruits, cherry tomato types and plants that are adaptable to container growing but which bear fruits of medium size.

Burpee's Pixie Hybrid—Especially developed for growing in containers. Only 14 to 18 inches tall; bears fruit larger than cherry tomato size; takes about 52 days from seed to fruit. A fine choice for a sunny winter windowsill.

Small Fry—An All-America Selection; bears large cherry-type fruit (about one inch in diameter) in clusters of seven or eight; takes about 65 days from seed to fruit; a compact plant which grows to a height of about 30 inches. Bright crimson fruit.

Tiny Tim (red)—True miniature in size and fruit (about three-quarters of an inch in diameter); plants grow only about 15 inches tall and 14 inches across; suitable for a pot or a sunny window box; ornamental as well as a good producer, it takes about 55 days from seed to fruit.

Tiny Tim (yellow)—Has the same characteristics (and is lovely in combination with) Tiny Tim (red).

Patio—Developed especially for growing in tubs and containers; reaches a height of 24 to 30 inches; fruit is of medium size, red, round, of excellent quality and flavor; takes 70 days from seed to fruit.

Tomato Sugar Lump—Bite-size fruit with unusually sweet flavor; takes about 65 days from seed to fruit. Deep green vines.

Burgess Early Salad Hybrid—Produces very early in the season as it requires only 45 days from seed to fruit; fairly short (10 to 12 inches) and produces an abundance of fruit about one and one-half inches in diameter.

Tomato Stakeless—Not specifically developed for container but does well. Grows to height of 18 to 24 inches; takes about 80 days from seed to fruit. The plant itself has thick, heavy, compact foliage. Fruit can average as much as 5 ounces in weight when container-grown.

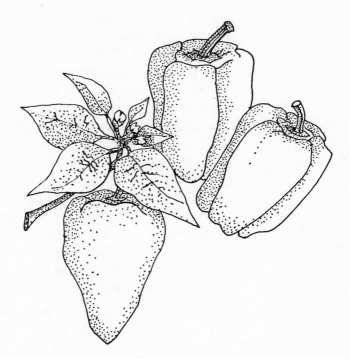

Green Peppers

Peppers are one of the most attractive crops a city gardener can grow. The sturdy plants are upright and symmetrically shaped, with dark green foliage. They bear a continuous crop of waxy green fruit, which ripens to red if left on the plant. After the plant begins bearing, you will have blossoms and fruit in all stages of maturity throughout the summer months.

Sow the seed in individual peat pots (as described on page 37) for best results, and transplant later—about eight weeks or so—into permanent containers. Peppers require a long, warm growing season and about the same cultural requirements as tomatoes and eggplant. These three crops, in fact, make an eye-catching trio, and they are among the most productive crops you can grow, for they can even make a small dent in the grocery bill.

Depending somewhat on the variety, you can harvest your first peppers about eight weeks after transplanting. And peppers needn't be full size for harvesting. Pick some of the smaller ones for use in salads while letting others reach full growth for stuffing and baking. Frequent picking will encourage production throughout the summer.

Like tomatoes, peppers can be brought in at the approach of frost. They will do quite nicely as houseplants in a sunny window, while all but the smallest fruit will finish out to maturity. The plant can also be pruned to keep it compact and carried over to the next year.

Bell Boy Hybrid—All-America Selection. Plants grow 18 to 24 inches; takes about 70 days from seed to fruit. Fruit groups near the crown of the plant, making it a good show-off for a crop in a pot. Fruit is sweet and mild; good for picking and eating on the spot.

Burgess Michigan Wonder—Produces large, fat peppers with thick flesh; takes 68 days from transplanting to fruit.

Parkwonder F₁ Hybrid—This sturdy plant is a dependable, heavy producer of medium-size fruit; takes 65 days from transplanting to fruit.

Canape—Early producer (only 62 days from transplanting to fruit); average-size fruit is two by three inches, and is sweet and mild; plant grows to a height of 20 to 25 inches.

Sweet Banana—A lovely, ornamental plant as well. The long pointed fruit appears as light green, turning yellow, then orange and finally to red as it matures. Looks like a hot pepper type but surprises you with a mild sweet taste. Compact plant bears lots of fruit; takes about 65 days from seed to fruit.

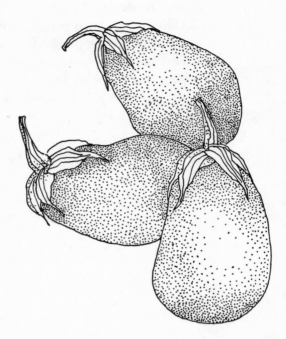

Eggplant   Eggplant is a joy to grow. The plant is as beautiful as its fruit. Its culture is similiar to that of tomatoes and green peppers. Plants require a long, warm growing season and should not be put outside until the weather is dependably warm. Eggplant seedlings are available in many garden supply houses at the same time of year (usually March or April) as tomato and green pepper plants. If you purchase seedlings, one or two (except for the midget variety) should be sufficient to produce all the fruits you are likely to use.

If you decide to raise plants from seed, do not be intimidated by reports of difficulty in germination or transplanting. Eggplants are just as easy to work with as tomatoes and are handled in the same man-

ner. Plant seeds eight to nine weeks before it's time
to put seedlings outside.

Depending upon the variety, the plants will grow
from two to three feet in diameter and be bushy or
flat as trained. They will begin to bear approximately 75 days after transplanting. As the blossoms appear (they are an attractive lavender),
pinch off a few to keep the eggplant from setting too
many fruits; about five or six per plant is best.
Terminal growths on the stems can also be pinched
back to maintain the shape of the plant—short and
bushy, or taller as desired.

Don't wait too long to harvest. You can use the
fruit any time after it is about half-grown. And don't
wait until it loses its glossy shine; by that time, the
fruit will have a tough texture and a slightly bitter
taste. Keep fruit picked to keep plant bearing.

Morden Midget (Park)—Short, sturdy, bushy
plants; small-size fruit—enough for one person as a
main dish, for two as an accompaniment; excellent
quality; the lustrous fruit nestling in gray-green
foliage makes a striking patio or porch accent.

Black Beauty—Longtime favorite of home gardeners; produces large, traditional-sized purplish
black fruit; plants grow into compact bushes and
are very productive; takes 73 days from setting out
of plants to maturity. Fruit will not be as large when
container-grown as what you are accustomed to
seeing in the market, so be sure to pick while still
glossy.

Lettuce

If you can't wait to taste, grow some lettuce. Of the three general types—crisphead, butterhead and loosehead (or leaf)—the leaf varieties are best for container gardening. They require a much shorter growing season than the solid-head varieties (40 to 50 days as compared with 70 to 80 days) and are easier to grow. Leaf lettuce also makes a most attractive pot plant, producing a beautiful array of greens with interesting shapes and textures.

Leaf lettuce needs no transplanting. The seed can be sown very early in the spring directly into the container or area where it is to mature. A light frost will not kill it, though it may slow growth. The lettuce produces "instant" crops. You can be eating its "thinnings" in about three weeks. Successive plantings made at 10-day intervals will supply tender thinnings for weeks. As the lettuce matures, choose mostly outer leaves along with a few of the inner ones each cutting. You won't believe the flavor of lettuce eaten the same day it's picked.

Usually, after about two months' growth, the leaves begin to toughen and the plants go quickly to seed. At this point, discard the plant entirely or keep it watered and cared for till the cool fall weather when it will reseed itself and produce a new crop of tender leaves. Remember, lettuce just can't take heat.

Salad Bowl—Frilly, curled leaves with long stems; resembles chicory or curly endive, but is light green; leaves are crisp and tender; grows high, wide and handsome in its container; takes about 48 days to mature.

Oak Leaf—Small-leaved, deep, compact plant; more heat-resistant than most varieties; not as frilly as other leaf lettuce, it forms more of a rosette and is extremely attractive; matures in about 40 days.

Black Seeded Simpson—Inner leaves of Simpson are almost white, outer leaves are broad and wavy and frilled at the edges; available in pre-planted kits as well as seed packets; matures in about 45 days.

Ruby—A conversation piece as well as good eating—bright green leaves are tinged with red; takes about 47 days to mature.

Bibb types—The choice of the gourmet-gardener; *Burpee Bibb* is good to try; *Tom Thumb,* a miniature butterhead, takes longer to mature, a little over two months; produces small, rosette-shaped plants.

Spinach   No one's indifferent toward spinach. You either
like it (raw or cooked) or you don't. But even those
who hate it on a plate will love it on a patio; spinach
makes a beautiful foliage plant with leaves of varied
textures and dark green color. It is a cool-season
crop and should be planted in early spring or late
summer. Where winters are mild, seed can be sown
in the fall, over-wintered and produced as an early
crop in the spring. Plan on a single plant for each
8- to 10-inch pot, and be sure to leave room for
several pots. Seed can be sown indoors in individual peat pots and transplanted to permanent
containers later; or it can be sown directly into the
permanent container.

For best flavor, spinach should be grown fast
(use a fertilizer high in nitrogen). When harvesting,
thin out leaves from each plant to keep the containers balanced and to encourage growth of the remaining plants.

Like other leaf crops, spinach needs plenty of

water. It cannot take heat at all (over 80 degrees is too hot), and if you want to grow greens through the summer, try Swiss chard or tampala as spinach substitutes.

Swiss chard is equally ornamental and is easier to grow than spinach. It is not discouraged by hot weather, where spinach will succumb. The leaves are large and crinkly and grow on long white or crimson stalks. Plant as for spinach, water generously, harvest the outer leaves only and it will produce through the summer.

Tampala is a spinachlike vegetable from China. Many gardeners prefer it to spinach for growing (it survives hot weather and produces all summer) and eating.

Bloomsdale—Leaves deeply crinkled; plant forms attractive rosettes of glossy, dark green leaves; takes 48 days from seed to maturity.

Malabar—Large, bright leaves that grow on a viny stem; can be trained to a fence; will survive hotter weather than most spinach; 70 days from seed to maturity.

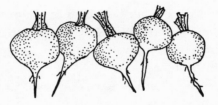

Radishes

Radishes are foolproof and fast. Sow the seeds in the container in which they will grow. Radishes must be grown fast—fertilize them at planting time and plan on a crop within three to four weeks. Give plants plenty of water to make them crisp and tender. Don't sow seeds too thickly and be sure to thin them out to at least an inch apart so that each radish will have room to develop. Radishes do well in artificial soil because it is light and the texture is consistent, and the developing root can expand at its ease.

Sow seeds early, as the plants cannot make it through the hot weather. A light frost will not hurt them. If you plan on more than one container, sow seeds a week or so apart so that they won't all mature at once. They must be eaten when mature or close to it, for they turn pithy quickly.

You can get two crops out of one container by a sort of reforestation plan—replace each radish when you pull it with another seed. Also, harvest every other radish to keep the foliage nicely balanced in the container. The foliage is decorative, producing something between a rosette and fountain effect. Try them around the rim of a large container, circling a planting of green onions.

Cherry Belle—Popular round, smooth, red

radish; crisp and tender; short tops make them good choice for container-growing; 24 days from seed to table.

Champion—A former All-America Selection; bright red; round shape; matures in 24 days.

Icicle—Pure white root shaped like its namesake; six inches long; mild, sweet and juicy; matures in 27 days.

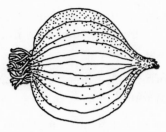

Onions

Most gardeners who grow onions like to start with "sets" or with very young plants instead of planting seed. Sets are small dry bulbs that can be bought by weight. A half-pound (one pint) will cost about 90¢ and contain 75 to 100 bulbs. The young plants are sold in bunches of 75 to 100 for about 75¢ if purchased at a local garden shop or nursery. They are slightly higher if ordered from a catalogue.

If you plan to harvest your crop as green onions (scallions), white sets and plants are preferable to yellow. Plant the sets or plants about an inch apart and not too deep (about one inch). Green onions from plants will be ready to eat in about three weeks; sets will take about five weeks. Harvest every other one so that the remaining onions will have room to develop larger bulbs.

If you are growing green onions from seed, Evergreen White Bunching seed is recommended. Each of these seeds sends up several shoots. You can pile soil around the shoot as it grows to keep it blanched white. These onions do not form bulbs. They require about four months from planting time to scallion size, although you can use them for flavoring within two months.

Onions can be planted very early in the spring. A light frost will not harm them. They enjoy full sun. Usually, no fertilizer is required.

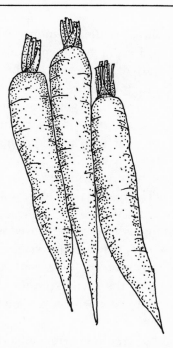

Carrots   Since carrots are always available in groceries, many city farmers discount them as a possible container crop. However, one taste of a tender baby carrot—two to three inches long and one-half inch in diameter—can be a whole new carrot experience, one worth savoring. Carrots are easy to grow and their fresh sweetness and texture are reward enough for the container space.

Artificial soil really comes into its own in raising carrots. Light, loose and free of lumps, it permits the rapid growth that carrots must have to be tender and sweet.

Carrot seed should be sown directly into its permanent containers. Make sure to coordinate the container with the variety of carrot grown, since carrot length will vary all the way from the three-inch Tiny Sweet to the six-inch Nantes. Obviously, you will need a planter deep enough to accommodate the length of the variety (or the length to which you will let it grow before harvesting) plus a couple of inches to spare. If your container is not deep enough, the carrot roots may just turn sideways and keep on growing, with underground chaos the result.

Seed can be sown in spring (up until very warm weather, actually) or fall. The soil needs to be kept moist during the germination period, which is sometimes as long as two or even three weeks. So it is a good idea after sowing the seed in damp soil to cover the top of the container with a sheet of plastic wrapping until the seeds sprout. Then remove the wrapping and water with a fine mist- or sprinkler-type can, as needed.

When the seedlings are about two inches tall, thin them to about an inch apart. An application of fertilizer at this time will help spur the fast growth essential for tender, juicy carrots. About four weeks later, the little baby carrots will have formed; thin the plants again to about three inches apart. This time, though, pull some to eat. The fresh flavor of these tender "thinnings" is a delightful taste treat; while you enjoy the early harvest, you will be giving the remainder of the plants room to develop to full maturity. Most varieties require 65 to 75 days to mature to full size.

Tiny Sweet—Midget variety; roots grow to three inches; ready to eat in two months; tender, crisp and sweet.

Short 'n Sweet—Grows three and one-half to four inches long and about two inches thick at the top; takes 68 days to mature.

Nantes Coreless—Matures to about six inches in 68 days; smooth, well-flavored carrot with practically no visible core.

Little Finger—A baby carrot, only about one half-inch round and three inches long; matures in about 65 days. Small tops mean more room in the pot for more plants.

Oxheart—This is a short, chunky carrot, almost as wide (three inches) as it is long (four inches); takes about 75 days to mature. Pull and eat while still young for sweetest flavor.

Gold Nugget—Another chunky little carrot, two to three inches long; matures in about 71 days. Crisp, sweet eating; great for relish trays.

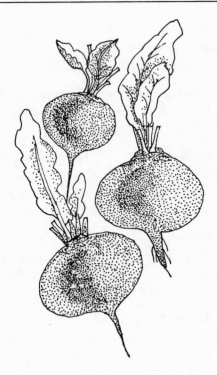

Beets

Beets are a practical container crop because the plant is completely edible. The beets themselves will be deliciously sweet and the tops can be used for salads or cooked greens.

Beet seeds are actually small balls (fruits) containing several seeds. Once planted, several seedlings emerge in a bunch. When the plants have grown to a height of two inches, they should be thinned to stand about one and one-half inches apart. After they reach about eight inches, they should be thinned again. Remove every other plant, leaving a three-inch space between plants. Don't let the beets themselves grow too large before final harvesting. Their flavor is best when they are young. Pull the vegetables when they are about one and one-half inches in diameter.

Beets prefer cool temperatures; sow early in the spring or in the fall. They have a way of heaving out of the soil as they grow; when they do, simply put a bit more earth on top to cover them.

The plants will do well in artificial soil. Their seedlings are small and weak, and the fine texture of artificial soil is an advantage; clods of real dirt interfere with the developing root.

Ruby Queen—Tops are short (10 to 12 inches) and make attractive pot plants; the root is round, smooth and bright red; fine texture makes tender delicious eating—pickled or cooked; matures in about 55 days.

Detroit Dark Red—Produces a deep dark red root; sweet-flavored and tender; good for greens, too; takes about 58 days to mature.

Burpee's Golden Beet—New variety has reddish, golden roots (beets); tops make good greens, cooked or fresh; beets are best when eaten small; matures in about 55 days; definitely unique.

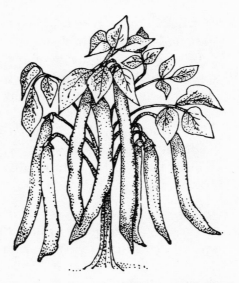

Bush Beans   Bush beans—both snap and lima—are the best
bean bet for container gardening. (Pole beans are
more productive but not as attractive.) The low-
growing bush beans can be lined up in a row for a
sort of "edible hedge" or stationed about the patio
to pose as "shrubs." The mature plants will be one
to two feet high, depending on the variety.

Plan on several pots if you have the space. Not
only will you dress up the patio, but you will be
able to harvest enough young beans from among the
plants for a meal. Eight to 10 bean bushes should
supply a family of two or three for several weeks.
Most varieties will provide five or six pickings over
the season. Pick the beans while they are young—
before the seeds begin to swell in the pod. Early
harvest not only ensures good flavor but also encourages productivity.

Lima beans do best in regions with a long growing season. If this poses a problem, choose the

small butter bean which requires less growing time. Beans also need warm weather. They will respond to lots of water and to fertilizer, especially when the pods begin to form. Give the seeds a head start by soaking them overnight in warm water before planting. Sow seeds in early spring directly into the container in which they are to mature, spacing them as indicated on the seed packet.

GREEN SNAP BEAN:

Tenderpod—Probably the favorite of home gardeners; tender, with marvelous flavor; beans are about four and one-half to five and one-half inches long; takes about 50 days to mature.

Tenderette—Dark green pods, about five and one-half to six inches long, straight and smooth; white seeds; entirely stringless; 55 days.

BUTTER LIMA:

Henderson Bush—Pick when young; each pod yields three to four small, flat, green beans; 65 days from seed to maturity.

ORNAMENTALS:

Royalty Purple—Lovely plants produce dark purple pods, which turn green after about two minutes' cooking; delicious, tender, stringless and beautiful—a great combination for the container gardener; takes about 51 days to mature.

Burgess Yard Long Bean—A "Gee Whiz" crop with bean pods three feet long. The vigorous vine will require staking and a railing or trellis to grow on; 70 days from seed to maturity. Full-sized beans can be shelled for use as dry beans; when young and small they can be eaten as snap beans.

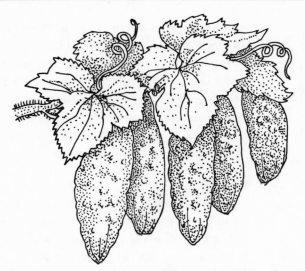

Cucumbers   Gardeners who are still a bit timid in the presence of tiny, frail sprouts will welcome cucumbers and their sturdy, robust, aggressive seedlings. Cucumbers make a strong statement from the minute they poke up out of the soil.

Cucumbers may be sown indoors in peat pots very early in the spring and transplanted to the permanent container outdoors after all danger of frost has passed. Or they may be sown indoors directly into the permanent container. The use of small individual peat pots merely allows you to handle more seedlings in a small area.

If you sow directly into the permanent container, plant in "hills" or "sets"—several seeds planted together. Six to eight seeds in the middle of a large container (and later thinned to three or four plants) will produce a generous display of vine and fruit.

The vines will trail unless trained. Put a piece of fencing in, or next to, the planter, or set the planter next to a railing or trellis. Train the vine early before fruit begins to set. If you're late in positioning the vines, you may expose the developing fruits to too much direct sun and they will shrivel and die.

Cucumbers left to develop normally will seek the protective shade of the leaves. In training the vine, allow the center stem to grow as high as the fence, railing or trellis. Then pinch it off to allow the lateral stems to develop and then train these sideways.

Cucumbers also do well in hanging baskets. The vines can be allowed to trail to the floor, or can be trained to a nearby trellis or railing. Remember, however, that cucumber tendrils will entwine around whatever they can reach, including a nearby plant—so provide a string or cord of some kind to train them away from their neighbors. The plants take from 55 to 70 days to mature, depending on the variety, and at what stage you prefer to harvest them. If you're partial to tiny, sweet pickles, harvest in about 40 days. Or, if you prefer them sliced in salads or as bread and butter pickles, just leave them on the vine until they reach the right size. The plants will continue to produce right up until frost, but will slow down and not bear at all during very hot weather.

Patio Pik—A compact, dwarf plant with fruit that sets early; takes about 51 days from seed to maturity. Medium green color, fruit grows four to six inches long.

Midget Cucumber—A small vine (only two feet long) for small places. Fruit four inches long; matures in about 55 days. A pickling type you can peel for salads.

Sweet Slice—A burpless variety, sweet and bitterfree. Produces over a long period; fruit 10 to 12 inches long; takes about 62 days to mature.

Park's Comanche—Long dark green fruit, excellent for slicing; matures in about 50 days. Vines hold up well with leaves retaining good green color through the season, providing nice backdrop for other plants on porch or balcony.

Burgess Green Ice—A fine slicing and salad cucumber. Thin skin, crisp, firm fruit up to 10 inches long; takes about 48 days to mature. Strong vines easy to train to grow along a trellis or railing.

China Hybrid—something different and delicious; a very long (10 to 12 inches), slender cucumber about one and one-quarter inches in diameter; matures in about 58 days; seeds are few and small, fruit is crisp; ideal for either salads or pickling; great for a trellis.

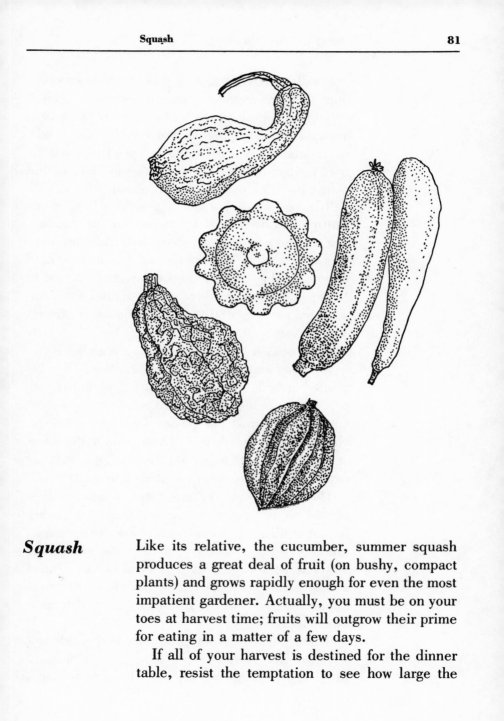

Squash   Like its relative, the cucumber, summer squash produces a great deal of fruit (on bushy, compact plants) and grows rapidly enough for even the most impatient gardener. Actually, you must be on your toes at harvest time; fruits will outgrow their prime for eating in a matter of a few days.

If all of your harvest is destined for the dinner table, resist the temptation to see how large the fruit will grow. They may double in size beyond the time they are at their prime. Since most farmers enjoy boasting about the size of the fruit they produce as well as quantity and quality, you might want to let a couple of squash go the limit, but for best eating, harvest while young—as soon as the skin can be pierced by the fingernail with practically no pressure. It's also a good idea to keep the fruit picked because it keeps the vine producing.

Zucchini can be harvested when fruits are only two inches or so long and about one-half inch in diameter. They are delicious cubed and sautéed in butter. Larger ones, three to five inches long, are good baked; larger still but not over-mature fruits, are marvelous sliced and fried.

Since squash is a member of the cucumber family, planting and culture are similar. Seeds can be planted indoors early in the spring in individual peat pots or outdoors in permanent containers after all danger of frost has passed. If sown outdoors, plant five or six seeds to a hill and thin to the three or four strongest-looking seedlings. Apply soluble fertilizer when the plants are about four inches tall.

The permanent container for squash plants should be as large as you can manage—a bushel basket or washtub, for example. Give the squash as much sun as possible—moving the containers about as needed. Squash roots should be kept moist almost continually, so mulch the top of the container with peat or spaghnum moss or shredded newspapers.

Winter squash grows as a vine, and if left untrimmed can overrun your balcony. Snip it back judiciously, sacrificing some of the crop to make room for other vegetables and for yourself. The fruit ripens in the fall and most recommendations (unlike those for summer squash) call for leaving the fruit on the vine until it is fully mature and the rind hardened. Actually, this is to allow the grower to store the squash through the winter because the fruit will not keep unless it is well-matured. The fruit can, however, be eaten before it reaches maturity. The flavor is good, although different from that of the mature fruit.

SUMMER SQUASH

Early White Bush—The leading scallop-type summer squash; takes about 54 days to mature; fruits grow to seven or eight inches across but are best harvested and eaten when three to four inches wide; flesh is white (and delicious).

Cocozelle and Zucchini—Both are bush summer squash introduced from Italy and are becoming enormously popular as interest in international cuisines increases. They take from 50 to 60 days to mature. *Early Cocozelle* has fruit 10 to 12 inches long; smooth dark green with faint light green stripes changing to yellow. *Chefini Hybrid,* a zucchini type, has dark green, slender, straighten cylindrical fruit. Strong sturdy bush.

Aristocrat—An All-America Selection, is another wonderful zucchini type, with smooth dark green fruit; matures in about 48 days. Strong, sturdy bush produces throughout the summer.

Baby Crookneck—Small compact bush; small yellow fruit; takes about 53 days to mature. Highly ornamental.

FALL AND WINTER SQUASH:

Gold Nugget—Round, bright orange fruit, enormous leaves and beautiful yellow flowers; bushlike growth habits make it excellent for containers; matures in about 95 days.

True Hubbard—Dark green, warted skin outside, deep orange-yellow flesh inside; takes a big container; fruit is larger than a football, weighs 10 to 12 pounds; 115 days from seed to maturity.

Bush Table King—An All-America Selection. Acorn type; fruits are five inches in diameter; dark green skin with pale orange flesh; delicious when baked; takes 85 days from seed to maturity.

Butternut—Skin is light buff color, flesh is pale orange; fruits are bottle-shaped, 10 to 12 inches long; sweet, nutty flavor; takes 95 days from seed to maturity.

Herbs

Interest in gourmet cooking has zoomed in recent years; not far behind is the gourmet-gardener growing his own herbs and snipping off leaves and stems at their peak of quality and flavor. Do-it-yourself kits now make herbs the easiest possible gardening project for an apartment resident. A selection of seeds, the pots and planting mix are all put together in one package. Such kits are widely available in specialty shops, department stores and gift catalogues as well as from the usual seed sources.

A typical kit contains 24 peat pots, potting soil and an assortment of seeds: basil, chives, dill, marjoram, oregano, parsley, sage and thyme. All of these plants are relatively easy to grow, and the kit is a painless and productive introduction to herb culture.

The herbs listed above, plus many others, are also available in separate seed packets from the seed companies and off the rack at the garden shops. (Parsley is usually listed in the vegetable section of the catalogue.) Many herbs are perennials (plants that reseed themselves and come up each year) and can grow to be old friends. Almost all varieties can be dried and stored. (Keep them in tightly closed glass containers out of strong light.)

Beginners who go beyond the pre-planted kits might start with seed of three annuals—dill, savory and borage. All germinate quickly from seed and can be sown where they are to grow—but sparingly. Extra plants should be pinched off at ground level. Parsley seed should be soaked in water for 24 hours before planting for faster germination. It doesn't pay to grow chives from seed; potted clumps are relatively inexpensive and often available at supermarkets.

You don't have to be a cook to be an herb fancier. Their foliage and fragrance are reward enough for the small space they take up. For a lovely aroma try lemon balm or lemon verbena, and the various mints, from spear to apple.

A strawberry jar with a variety of herbs peeking from its pockets will make an intriguing and useful "garden accompli" indoors or out. Most herbs love sun, so a south or west window usually suits them best. Gourmet gardeners who want their herbs close at hand on the kitchen counter should plan on a double row of fluorescent lights under the kitchen cabinet and the pots of herbs placed so that they are within a foot or less of the lights. Flat fluorescent fixtures that fit snugly under a kitchen cabinet and that can be plugged into an outlet are widely available at hardware stores. They are relatively inexpensive and well worth the small cost and effort to provide a seasoning shelf of live herbs at your fingertips.

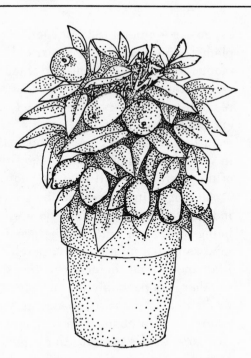

Citrus

City gardeners can have the best of both worlds, the houseplant and the edible crop, with a dwarf citrus tree. Try oranges, lemons or limes. Gorgeous foliage, fragrant blossoms, colorful and delicious fruit and limited culture requirements make citrus a favorite of almost everyone who has grown it.

Citrus trees *can* be started from seeds of fruit purchased at the grocery. However, novices often have difficulty in getting these seeds to germinate. If the seeds do sprout, the plants do not always bloom; if blooming stage is reached, fruit does not always set; and, finally, if fruit does grow, it is rarely "true" to the fruit which produced the seed. Forget it! Purchase citrus plants from the garden shop or order them from a catalogue. They are not expensive—around $2.50 each for one-year-old plants; $5 each for two-year-old (bearing age) plants. The year-old plants are about a foot tall; the two-year-old plants about two feet tall. They can reach a height of six or seven feet, or they can be cut back and maintained at three or four feet or even less. Once they are established, they can be in various stages of flowering and fruiting for much of the year. They will bear for years and years.

Although citrus trees can be grown successfully indoors (all the time), they do seem to appreciate being outside in mild weather; and they can certainly smarten up a balcony, porch or patio. If you like, move them outdoors in the spring after the weather is dependably warm. Follow the procedure for hardening plants by managing the shift without sudden, sharp changes in temperature, and over-exposure to direct sun. Don't put them out, for example, until the temperature is close to what they have been accustomed to indoors; 60- to 70-degree weather would be about right. For a gradual adjustment, leave them out for a few hours at a time, bringing them back in before the temperature gets too hot or drops too low. And shade them from the direct sun until they are used to it.

If you must keep a citrus tree indoors the year round, put it in your sunniest window. Rotate the tree about once a week so that all sides get exposure to the sun. This will encourage the balanced development of the tree as well as the growth of blossoms and fruit. The trees should also be kept away from radiators or heat ducts.

Citrus trees require a lot of water and should be fertilized every three to four weeks while they are bearing fruit (which is for a good part of the year). Also, give them just a pinch of chelated iron once a month. The trees prefer a humid atmosphere, and to combat the dry heat common to apartments, fill a tray with gravel, keep it wet continuously and put the citrus container on the tray. If you have more than one plant, group them together under these same conditions. The more water around to evaporate, the better.

The plants will profit from an occasional bath. Use a warm, slightly soapy cloth to carefully wipe each leaf both top and underside. This not only rids the leaves of accumulated dust that clogs their breathing apparatus, but also helps ward off scale (a major pest of citrus) and other insect damage. If you set the whole plant in the shower, be sure the shower head is adjusted to a fine mist, otherwise the force of the water will dislodge the soil. Let the leaves dry before putting the plant back in direct sunlight.

An added note about scale: Should you spot a sticky-looking substance on the leaves of the plant, scale is likely to be the culprit. Turn the leaf over, and if you look closely you will see one or several tiny, round, light brown "spots." This is scale. Look closely because when the scale is attached along the main vein of the leaf it is sometimes hard to see.

A shower won't take care of this problem. Use a warm, soapy cloth and clean each leaf—gently loosening each scale as you go. The job may take 10 to 15 minutes, but it is time well-spent to keep the plant healthy. Usually, the chore need not be repeated; if at all, only every few weeks.

Here are some space-saving varieties suitable for indoor "groves":

Calamondin Orange—This tree tends to grow tall and columnar; it produces an abundance of blossoms and fruit, often in different stages of maturity at the same time; small, waxy, green leaves; oranges develop one to one-and one-half inches in diameter.

Tahiti Orange—Miniature tree, miniature fruit (one to two inches in diameter), delicate shiny green foliage.

Ponderosa Lemon—Leaves are larger than the Calamondin orange and lighter green in color; bears full-size fruit; a single lemon is often three to four inches in diameter, and weighs more than three pounds (one is enough for a large pie); blossoms are small, waxy and trumpet-shaped in especially fragrant clusters.

Persian Lime—Foliage similar to the Ponderosa lemon; full-size, bright green fruit.

Dwarf Peaches and Nectarines

With the genetic dwarfs now on the market you can grow delectable peaches and nectarines at home. These miniature trees make handsome ornamental plants, growing not much more than five feet tall. Fruits are full-size, however. And you can enjoy fruit from mid to late summer.

Order the trees for spring planting. They will probably be shipped in late February or early March and will arrive bare-rooted; they will also be accompanied by good, clear instructions on planting and care. (Before planting, check the sections in this book on selecting containers and preparing them for proper drainage. The potting mixture should be half garden soil and half peat moss.) Keep your tubbed tree in the shade at first, gradually moving it to full exposure. Use a mulch (a protective layer on top of the soil) of peat or sphagnum moss to help keep the soil from drying out.

Peach and nectarine trees, being deciduous, shed their leaves every fall and enter a dormant period until the following spring. To be productive, a peach or nectarine tree must be exposed to a certain amount of cold. Therefore, if you live in an area where winters are very mild, your tree may never become dormant and thus fail to produce fruit. If you live in a cold-winter area, the tree will have to be protected during periods of prolonged subfreezing temperatures. Fruit trees in containers will need to have their roots, as well as tops, protected from the cold. An ideal covering is a large cardboard carton such as those used to ship refrigerators, televisions and other large appliances. Most stores are happy to give these away. Put a thick layer of newspapers under the container, and several layers around the sides, held in place with cord. Then just upend the carton over all.

Give the tree one last good soaking after cold weather comes but before the long, hard winter sets in. Then let it take the first freeze or so with the container part protected only by the layers of newspapers (these can be kept dry with a plastic covering if necessary). Now, move the tree to a sheltered location (a corner of the balcony, for example) pop the carton over it and add no more water until spring. Begin watering again as soon as the soil thaws, but beware of the late spring frost and do not remove the protective insulation too early.

PEACHES

Burpee Golden Glory—Grows five to six feet high and four to five feet across. Fruit is large, freestone.

Stark Golden Treasure—Bushlike ornamental tree under six feet tall. Fruit up to two and one-half inches across.

NECTARINES

Burpee Golden Prolific—Grows five to six feet tall; juicy, freestone fruit ripens in mid- to late-August.

Stark Sunburst—Bushlike growth to tree; fruit is highly colored, juicy, semi-freestone.

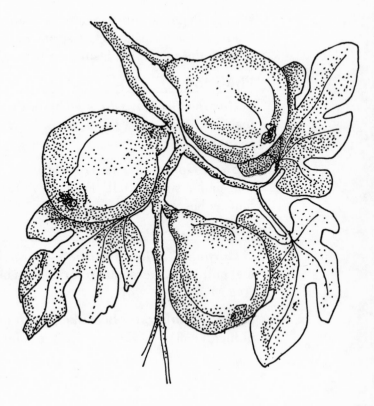

Figs

Fig trees require only a minimum of care and will provide lots of fruit for eating and preserving. They need six to eight hours of sunlight a day, so would fare best on the patio or balcony.

They should be brought in for the winter and literally stored away. Since this is their resting period, they need very little light or water, but they should have a reasonably low temperature, certainly lower than ordinary room temperature. An unheated attic, cellar or garage is a good place; in an apartment, possibly a room set aside for the tenant's storage needs. If you have an area that you can keep on the cool side and want to try to over-winter the tree, plan to bring it in before the heat goes on.

If there is no suitable storage space and your winters are not too severe, you might try overwintering your fig tree outside. It must be sheltered from both frost and wind. Gardeners are always being told to mulch their plants with straw or hay to protect them from the cold, but in the city, these products are difficult to find. Shredded newspaper will work as mulch, but it disintegrates if it gets wet. If the tree is placed under a sheltering roof where it can be kept dry, newspaper is worth a try. Cut it into strips and then crumple it together. Pack the shredded newspapers on the soil around the base of the plant up to the first limbs. Dampen the newspaper slightly, to pack it more firmly around the base of the tree. A two- or three-inch layering of the plastic peanuts used as packing material also makes a good top covering over the newspaper mulch. In the spring, remove the mulch and resume watering to bring the plant into active growth.

Everbearing—Better for northern areas; very sweet fruit, perfect for eating fresh or for preserves; ripens in July or before frost begins.

Brown Turkey—Only for southern climates; medium-size, bronze fruit, ripens in mid-July.

Strawberries Strawberries provide an interesting challenge for the city gardener. The challenge is in the planting; the berries are actually easy to grow and require minimum care. New methods and equipment developed with the limited-space gardener in mind are a great aid in producing this luscious fruit.

There are two kinds of strawberries to grow: the everbearing varieties, which produce one crop in the autumn of the year in which they are planted, and additional crops in the spring and fall of the following year; and the June-bearing varieties which do not bear fruit until the year after planting. Although June-bearing varieties generally give the better crop, they produce no crop at all the first year. For this reason, city growers will probably be more satisfied—at least, less impatient—with one of the everbearing varieties. Whichever variety you choose, plant it in the spring as early as the seed house delivers or as soon as the plants reach garden supply stores.

Several types of containers are available for growing a number of strawberry plants in a small space. Probably the most ambitious is a pyramid-type planter. It is really a set of three five-inch-deep galvanized aluminum rings, the largest approximately six feet in diameter, and the second and third in descending size. (They are stacked atop each other in pyramid fashion.)

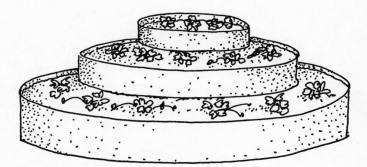

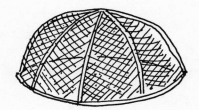

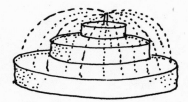

To prepare for planting, fill the first ring with soil, center the second ring on top of it, fill with soil, then add the third ring and fill it. This triple-level planter will accommodate as many as 50 plants. It is equipped with sprinkler, tubing and hose connections; optional accessories include a plastic cover to protect plants from frost, and a net screen to protect the berries from an over-enthusiastic flock of feathered fans.

If you can't spare a six-foot space for the berries, try a "strawberry jar." These are clay, pottery or ceramic vases with openings (pockets) in the sides where strawberry plants (herbs, succulents and other plants, too) may be tucked in. The jars can be found at garden stores, and in some flower shops and department stores. They usually cost about $5 to $10.

Strawberry barrels are another possibility and are most attractive on a patio or balcony. Ordinary wooden kegs can sometimes be found at lumber yards or hardware stores. Have the sides of the barrel drilled with one-inch diameter holes approximately eight inches apart (best in staggered rows) to accommodate the plants. (If you don't have access to a drill, ask to have this done at the lumber store. They'll most likely be willing to do the job for you and for only a small charge.) Place the barrel in what will be its permanent spot; after it is filled with dirt and planted, it will be too heavy for you to move.

Place about a two-inch layer of coarse gravel in the bottom of the barrel for drainage. Now take a mailing tube or a hollow pipe or a piece of fairly stiff plastic rolled into a two-inch wide cylinder and stand it in the middle of the barrel. Fill the tube with gravel and keep it in place while you begin filling the barrel with the richest soil you have. Tuck the strawberry plants (from the outside in, roots first) into each hole as the soil level reaches it. Water as you go along. This will settle the soil and prevent the whole thing from slumping in later on. Continue until the barrel is filled and then space a few more plants on top. Now you can remove the cylinder from the center. The gravel core that remains will help water drain down through the barrel and out to the plants.

On a still smaller scale, a dozen plants in a two-foot-square planter will produce some memorable "berries for breakfast" for a family of two or three.

It is important to plant strawberries at the proper

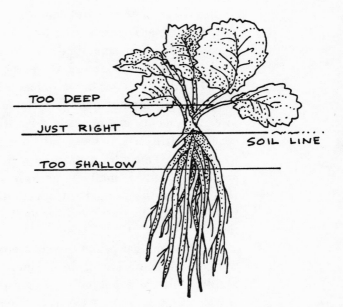

TOO DEEP

JUST RIGHT

SOIL LINE

TOO SHALLOW

depth—not too deep, not too shallow. Proper planting depth is at the level of the "crown"—an easily
seen point which divides the tops from the roots.

After the plants are well established and begin to
put out new growth, add a little soluble fertilizer to
the water you give them. To help develop strong
plants, pick off all flowers that appear until about
the first of July (if you have the everbearing variety). Your plants should begin to bear about a month
later. June-bearing varieties will begin to bloom in
late April and May, but remember there will be no
crop the first season they are planted.

Strawberries need too much sun to be grown successfully indoors but they can be wintered over
outdoors. As the weather grows cold, the plants will
begin to grow dormant. They can withstand frost
and light freezes, but should be protected against

hard freeze and severe weather. Covering the entire container with a tarpaulin will afford protection against cold; remove it when the weather warms.

Ozark Beauty—Everbearing; lush foliage; large, bright scarlet-red berries of good, sweet flavor.

Ogallala—Everbearing variety descended from the wild strawberry; combines hardiness with large berries of good flavor.

Surecrop—June-bearing variety; dependable and easy to grow; firm, deep rich red berry.

Kelly's Sparkle—June-bearing; big, sweet and juicy. Can be planted close together in a patch and make a good choice for a barrel.

Asparagus   Although asparagus provides more fun than food when planted in a container, don't let that keep you from trying. Asparagus is an interesting, easy plant to raise in a container and a real conversation piece. Plant several roots and plan on a party to celebrate the harvest of your crop a couple of years hence. You'll have to admit that such an event would classify as special!

Up until the last few years, asparagus roots were sold mainly through seed houses and nurseries, and usually in quantities of 25 roots or more. Today, you can often find them at local garden stands, packaged in quantities of as few as six. If you don't want but have room for six containers of asparagus, then share with a friend.

The root itself is interesting; thick, white tendrils stretch out like an octopus from a center crown. The roots need to be spread out when planted, so you will need a large container. One 14 inches across the top and 11 inches deep will house one root. (Plastic trash baskets make inexpensive containers.)

Asparagus likes a rich diet, so to your ordinary potting mix, you should add, per pot, an extra couple of tablespoons of a 5-10-5 fertilizer and a helping of cow manure. (Packaged dry cow manure can be found in garden centers or can be ordered through garden supply catalogs. It is to be mixed with water to form what is known in garden circles as manure "tea" and should be applied according to label directions. Packaged manure, enough to mix with water to make three gallons, costs about 65 cents; enough for 20 gallons about $3.00.) In addition, the plants should be fed about every other week with your regular plant food.

The first spring after planting, only one or two asparagus spears will come up. Don't cut these. They will grow up tall, as high as four to six feet, filming out into feathery fern. In late summer, berries form on the ferns, and their bright orange-red color adds to the beauty of the plant.

As winter approaches, the plant dies down. Give a final watering with manure tea and then hold off on any more water. Asparagus must have a dormant, or resting, period. Gardeners in the southern parts of the country where winters are warm and moist will not have luck with this vegetable.

As for severe winters, you can protect the roots from freezing by placing the pot in a sheltered spot, and/or by wrapping the pot around with newspaper covered with plastic. Asparagus is a sturdy crop, and you will be able to take it through the winter with this simple protection.

The second year, and each succeeding year in the spring, feed again with 5-10-5 and liquid manure. You can begin harvesting the stalks as they appear. Don't let them grow more than eight inches in height. If you have one container, you'll get only a few spears at a time, enough for a small side dish. Or, you can blanch them in hot water for three to five minutes and freeze till you have enough for a meal. With several containers, you can have enough cuttings for that special asparagus party. The same roots will go on producing for 20 years or more, so once you start asparagus you can plan on a long-time, meaningful relationship with this plant!

Mary Washington—is by far the most widely available variety.

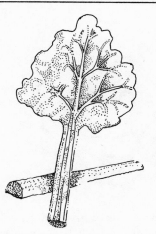

Rhubarb   Rhubarb makes a beautiful container plant. Handle much like asparagus, although the roots should be set a bit deeper, three to four inches under the top of the soil. Let the plant grow for a couple of years before taking cuttings of the stalks. Choose the fattest ones to cut and leave the skinny ones for the plant. Rhubarb stalks when grown in a pot can reach an inch in diameter; the same type of plant grown in the garden in full sun might produce stalks up to two inches in diameter. However, only a stalk or two of rhubarb when combined with fresh strawberries is a treat worth growing. And in the meantime, rhubarb will make a large, dramatic ornamental plant. Huge green leaves and scarlet stalks make it an eye-stopper. In the fall, the plant will die down and go dormant for the winter. Protect the roots from freezing temperatures as with asparagus.

Cabbage

Cabbage is an unlikely and therefore highly entertaining crop to grow in a container! One cabbage to a eight- to ten-inch container will allow the head to grow to full size. A wide bushel basket can accommodate a whole ring of one of the smaller varieties. (Plant carrots in the middle.)

Start cabbage seed six weeks before the last frost date in spring; sow several seeds to each pot or spot. After the seeds sprout and grow to an inch or so, select the strongest seedling and prune out the others.

The main nemesis of cabbage is the same as that for spinach or lettuce: heat. It is therefore best to choose early varieties that will develop before full summer comes on. The early varieties also require less space. Cabbages must have excellent drainage, lots of water, and regular feeding.

In harvesting, cut the heads so that a few inches of stalk are left, and you will likely encourage new growth of a small loose head or two that can make a welcome addition to a salad or sandwich.

Burnett's Baby-Head—Small, perfectly round, tender heads. Reaches maturity in about six weeks.

Park's Earliana—Small, round head, about five inches across; matures in about 60 days. Attractive as a container plant.

Dwarf Morden—A firm, round ball, four inches across and weighing only a pound. Lovely smooth leaves with light veining.

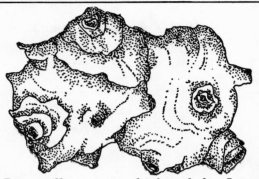

Jerusalem Artichokes

Practically no one thinks of the Jerusalem artichoke as a container plant, and yet the yield per pot (better, a tub) is as high as for any crop with the possible exception of the tomato. It is easy to grow and one plant produces a number of potato-like tubers that can be baked, boiled, creamed, pickled or eaten raw.

The Jerusalem artichoke is a relative of the sunflower, grows as high as six feet, with bright yellow blossoms two to three inches across in late summer. When the plant begins to die down, the tubers can be dug up. (Leave at least one in the pot, mulch for the winter, and expect a new plant in the spring.)

While the tubers look a good deal like potatoes, they have a somewhat nutty flavor and can substitute for water chestnuts in Chinese dishes. When steamed and creamed, they have a delicate flavor not unlike cauliflower. They do not store as well as potatoes, so they should be dug up only as they are to be used.

GROWTH CHART

Crop	Container Requirements	Growing Season
BEETS	Any allowing soil depth of 10 to 12 inches	cool weather— early spring, fall
BUSH BEANS (snap or lima)	Any having 8 to 10 inches of soil	warm weather
CABBAGE	8 to 10 inches wide 6 inches deep	cool weather— early spring
CARROTS	Any with depth of variety selected plus 2 inches (10 to 12 inches of soil usually ample)	cool weather— early spring, fall
CUCUMBERS	Gallon size for one plant; 5 gallon size for 3 or 4 plants; hanging basket good for single plant	warm weather
EGGPLANT	Not less than 3-gallon size; use 12 to 14 inch diameter pot for each plant	warm weather
GREEN PEPPER	Not less than gallon size per plant	warm weather
LETTUCE	Any type container suitable; size determined by quantity	cool weather; can stand light frost
ONIONS	Any type container suitable; should be 8 to 10 inches deep for green onions	cool weather; can stand light frost
RADISHES	Any type container suitable; should be at least 6 inches deep	cool weather; can stand light frost
SPINACH	An 8- to 10-inch pot per plant	cool weather— early spring, fall
SQUASH	At least 5-gallon size for each 3-or 4-plant "hill" (bushel basket, garbage can & washtub are practical)	warm weather; will produce through fall
TOMATOES	Dwarf types in gallon size; standard varieties need 2- to 3-gallon size; miniatures can make it in an 8- to 10-inch pot.	warm weather

For specific information developed by your state climatologist on average last and first frost dates for your area, check with your local Weather Service Office (some

Where to Make Initial Planting	When to Make Initial Planting	Days From Seed to Harvest	Approximate Average Size of Mature Plant
directly into container	2 to 4 weeks before frost-free date	50 to 60	10 to 12 inches tall
directly into container	early spring	snap 50 to 55 lima 65	1 to 2 feet tall
in peat pots for early start	6 weeks before last frost date	45 to 60 days	4 to 6 inches for midget sizes
directly into container	2 to 4 weeks before frost-free date	65 to 75	10 to 12 inches tall
in peat pots for early start	3 to 4 weeks before frost-free date	55 to 70	vines can be shaped by pinching back
in peat pots for early start	8 to 9 weeks before transplant time	120 to 140	2 to 3 feet tall
in peat pots for early start	7 to 8 weeks before frost-free date	110 to 120	2 to 3 feet tall
directly into container	4 to 6 weeks before frost-free date	40 to 50	6 to 10 inches tall
directly into container	4 to 6 weeks before frost-free date	35 to 45 days from sets to green onion	10 to 12 inches tall
directly into container	2 to 4 weeks before frost-free date	24 to 30	6 to 8 inches tall
directly into container	2 to 4 weeks before frost-free date	50 to 70	plants spread out, grow only a few inches tall
in peat pots for early start	3 to 4 weeks before frost-free date	summer: 50 to 60 winter: 85 to 110	bush type: 2 to 3 feet tall vine type: controlled by pinching off ends of runners
in peat pots	6 to 8 weeks before frost-free date	50 to 80, depending on type	dwarf type: 2 to 3 feet tall standard varieties: 3 to 5 feet tall

300 offices around the country), listed in the phone book under U. S. Government, Department of Commerce.

CATALOGUES

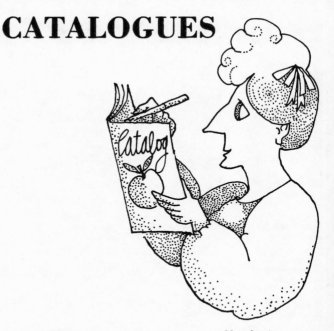

Archias' Seed Store P.O. Box 109 106 East Main St. Sedalia, Mo. 65301	*vegetables, berries, garden aids, herbs*
Burgess Seed & Plant Co. Galesburg, Mich. 49053	*vegetables, berries garden aids, dwarf fruit, herbs*
Burnett Brothers, Inc. 92 Chambers St. New York, N.Y. 10007	*vegetables garden aids, herbs*
W. Atlee Burpee Co. Warminster, Pa. 18974 or Riverside, Calif. 92502 or Clinton, Iowa 52732	*vegetables, berries, garden aids, dwarf fruit, herbs*
Burrell Seed Growers Co. Rocky Ford, Colo. 81067	*vegetables, peat pots*
DeGiorgi Company, Inc. Seed Growers & Importers P.O. Box 413 Council Bluffs, Iowa 51501	*vegetables*
Farmer Seed & Nursery Co. Fairbault, Minn. 55021	*vegetables, berries, garden aids, herbs*

Henry Field Seed & Nursery Co. Shenandoah, Iowa 51602	*vegetables,* *garden aids, berries, herbs*
Gurney Seed & Nursery Co., Inc. Yankton, S. Dak. 57078	*vegetables, berries,* *garden aids*
Kelly Bros. Nurseries, Inc. Dansville, N. Y. 14437	*berries,* *dwarf fruit, herbs*
Krider Nurseries, Inc. Middlebury, Ind. 46540	*vegetables, berries,* *herbs*
J. W. Jung Seed Co. Randolph, Wisc. 53956	*vegetables, berries,* *garden aids, herbs*
Earl May Seed & Nursery Co. Shenandoah, Iowa 51603	*vegetables, berries,* *garden aids, herbs*
The Meyer Seed Co. 600 So. Caroline St. Baltimore, Md. 21231	*vegetables, berries,* *garden aids, herbs*
Midwest Seed Growers 505 Walnut St. Kansas City, Mo. 64106	*vegetables*
Neosho Nurseries Neosho, Mo. 64850	*berries*
L. L. Olds Seed Co. P.O. Box 1069 Madison, Wisc. 53701	*vegetables, garden aids*
Geo. W. Park Seed Co., Inc. Greenwood, S.C. 29646	*vegetables* *garden aids, herbs*
Rayner Brothers, Inc. Salisbury, Md. 21801	*vegetables* *berries*
R. H. Shumway Seedsman Rockford, Ill. 61101	*vegetables, berries* *garden aids, dwarf fruit*
Stark Bros. Nurseries & Orchards Louisiana, Mo. 63353	*berries,* *dwarf fruit*
George Tait & Sons, Inc. 900 Tidewater Drive Norfolk, Va. 23516	*vegetables, garden aids*
Wetsel Seed Company, Inc. P.O. Box 791 Harrisonburg, Va. 22801	*vegetables,* *garden aids, herbs*

HOME GROWING RECORD

Date Planted	Type & Variety Planted

Progress	*Date Harvested*	*Results*

Date Planted	Type & Variety Planted

Progress	Date Harvested	Results

Date Planted	*Type & Variety Planted*

Progress	Date Harvested	Results

Books For People Who Like To Do Things For Themselves

Farming in a Flowerpot by Alice Skelsey $2.75
 How to Grow Fruits and Vegetables in Small Containers

Soap by Ann Bramson $2.75
 Making It, Enjoying It

Putting Up Stuff for the Cold Time by Crescent Dragonwagon $2.45
 Canning, Preserving & Pickling

Wine-Making at Home by Bruce Palmer $2.75
 Crushing, Fermenting, Aging and Bottling Your Own Wine

The Bean Book by Crescent Dragonwagon
 Cooking, Planting, Growing, Harvesting, Drying, Eating & Just Thinking About Them

Potpourri, Incense and Other Fragrant Concoctions by Ann Tucker $2.45

How to Make Your Own Hammock & Lie in It by Denison Andrews $2.45

Gardener's Diary by Joan Lee Faust $2.45
 For Recording the Growth of Your Garden

Nostalgia Crafts Book by Phyllis Fiarotta $5.95

Needlepoint from America's Great Quilt Designs by Mary Kay Davis and Helen Giammattei $5.95

Books For Parents And Children Who Like To Do Things Together

Sticks & Stones & Ice Cream Cones by Phyllis Fiarotta $4.95
 The Crafts Book for Children

Toybook by Steven Caney $3.95
 More than 50 Toys to Make with Children

Growing Up Green by Alice Skelsey and Gloria Huckaby $4.95
 Parents and Children Gardening Together

Making Children's Furniture and Play Structures by Bruce Palmer $3.95

These books are available at local book stores or by writing directly to the publisher (enclose 35¢ for handling and postage).
 Workman Publishing Company
 231 East 51st Street   New York, New York 10022